Charles J L

HIGHLAND BOOKSHOP
FORT WILLIAM

Butterfly Watching

Butterfly Watching

Paul Whalley

With drawings by
Richard Lewington

SEVERN HOUSE NATURALIST'S LIBRARY

To Mary

The author would like to record his grateful
thanks to Heather Angel for contributing
the section on photographing butterflies.

Richard Lewington wishes to record his
thanks to Brian Baker of Reading Museum
for his help with the loan of specimens.

British Library Cataloguing in Publication Data

Whalley, Paul Ernest Sutton
  Butterfly watching. – (Severn House Naturalist's Library).
  1. Butterflies – Great Britain –
  Observers' manuals
  1. Title
  595.7'89'072041   QL555.G7
  ISBN 0-7278-2002-8

Published by Severn House Publishers Limited
144–146 New Bond Street
London W1Y 9FD

Text © Paul Whalley 1980
Drawings © Severn House Publishers Limited 1980

ISBN 0 7278 2002 8

Filmset by Tameside Filmsetting Limited, Ashton-under-Lyne, Lancashire

Printed and bound by New Interlitho SpA, Milan, Italy

Contents

1 Butterflies and Man

One of the reasons for writing a book on butterfly watching is the desire to stimulate interest in a neglected area of natural history. Butterflies have been collected for many years and a great deal is known about their distribution and life-histories. It is difficult, however, to answer questions like 'Where do butterflies roost at night?' or, 'Which butterflies have territories and how do they defend them?' To answer these and other queries about their behaviour, and to obtain as complete a picture of butterfly life as possible, we need a little time from a lot of people who will look a little harder at a butterfly next time they see one, and perhaps begin to keep a few notes about its behaviour.

In natural history there is a great tradition of the gradual accumulation of knowledge by the amateur naturalist. The present-day birdwatchers are the descendants of the earlier naturalists who collected birds. These early collectors provided the basic information for both the scientists and the interested birdwatcher, and today's enthusiasts provide information on behaviour, migration, breeding and numbers, each person according to his own time and particular interests. Similarly, early collectors of butterflies have given us basic information about butterfly anatomy and distribution, but the questions to ask now are 'What is the butterfly doing?' and 'Why is it doing it?' The answers to such questions can only be found by watching butterfly behaviour in the field.

Butterflies are so much a part of the countryside that few people give them a second glance. Even the lepidopterists who collect them are periodically chided in their scientific journals about this. 'One would like to see so many more papers in the *Record* devoted not merely to accounts of breeding moths and butterflies from egg to pupa but to the actual habits of the living insect . . .' wrote P.S.M. Allen in 1967 in the monthly *Entomologist's Record*.

Recent studies on butterfly behaviour have shown that some species mark their own territories, many have complicated courtship displays and others migrate. In fact butterflies display all the habits normally associated with birds and with which birdwatchers are familiar, and the comparison of butterfly watching with birdwatching provides an interesting parallel. Butterfly watching has many features to commend it, not the least being that there is so much to find out about the subject. It is possible to get much closer to butterflies than to birds and although binoculars are useful for watching butterflies, they are not the essential tool they are for the birdwatcher. A small bonus for the butterfly watcher is the association of butterflies with warm, sunny days. The stoicism of the birdwatcher helping in a duck count in a freezing estuary is rarely called for in the butterfly watcher! I am not implying that an interest in butterflies is more appropriate for those too frail for birdwatching. The dedicated butterfly watcher will hunt for mountain species and for those to be found only in remote places, and the interest can become a full time ecological and behavioural study.

The aesthetic appeal of butterflies and their association with summer is perhaps matched by their 'marvellous transformation' as an eighteenth century authoress referred to it. The appeal of the 'ugly duckling' syndrome, the change from the earth-bound worm-like caterpillar to the beautiful butterfly, is familiar to us all and has been described in verse and prose through the ages.

Many of the commoner European butterflies can be easily recognised in the field. After a little practice and reference to illustrations in the field guides, the main family differences will be clear, and a good close-up view of the butterfly will enable it to be identified. From then on it is the behaviour we are interested in. In fact, it is quite reasonable to study a particular butterfly and its behaviour without worrying about its identification, just as individual birds or bird songs are recognised as distinct from others but not identified straight away. However, it is obvious from the illustrations in field guides that the identification of some butterflies needs close examination of, for example, the underside of the hindwing. Other butterflies may need to be netted for closer scrutiny and then released, in the same way that birdwatchers mist-net birds for identification and weighing before releasing them. A few species, especially from continental Europe, are very difficult (almost impossible) to identify in the field and these can be left to the dedicated enthusiast. None of the British butterflies come into this last category although there are some challenging species like the Essex and Small Skippers, or the female Brown Argus and female Silver-studded Blue. Most of the species in Britain are fortunately very distinctive and in the 'difficult' groups we often have only one species, compared with three or four of those in the rest of Europe.

Butterfly watching touches upon other branches of natural history such as sketching, photography and gardening, and the scope for those interested in any of these aspects to broaden their interest, both in the butterflies and in their own particular topic, is immense. The reaction of butterflies to birds, for example, has been little studied and needs the co-operation of birdwatchers. Eyespots on the wings of butterflies and bright wing colours are designed to frighten or dissuade birds from eating the butterflies. How successful are they? More botanical studies of butterflies and plants are needed. Butterflies recognise the plants on which they should lay their eggs. What particular flowers are butterflies attracted to for nectar or egg-laying, and at which stage are the flowers

Figure 1 This famous Egyptian tomb painting, 'Hunting scene in the Marshes', illustrates a few butterflies as if they have been disturbed by the hunters. They probably represent *Charaxes* species.

attractive? The co-evolution of butterflies and flowers has been the subject of many scientific papers and symposia. Apart from any importance in pollination, how do the butterflies react to the flowers in the wild? Do isolated flowers attract them less than a mass of blooms? Finding the answers to these and many other related problems will lead the botanist to take more notice of butterflies.

Sketching can be as important a part of watching butterflies as you care to make it. A few sketches of the insect's behaviour at a flower, or showing its reaction to other butterflies, can be of great help later when descriptions are written up in notes. The same is true of photographs. The photographer's pictures of habits and behaviour can be studied later surrounded by field guides, and this is a good way of confirming the identification of puzzling species.

An awareness of the activities of these beautiful insects in the field will lead you to notice them in illustrations and works of art. Has the artist used them for decorative purposes, as anonymous winged creatures, or can you identify actual species from the paintings?

Butterflies have been on the earth for much longer than Man. By the

8

time Man arrived on the scene, they were a well-established feature of the environment. Butterflies appear in the temperate zones at the onset of spring and it is tempting to think that Man associated them with other signs of this time of the year. Like the Cuckoo and Swallows they would have been a welcome sight after the winter months, and their colours would have attracted attention even in very early times.

The first records of butterflies occur in early Chinese and Egyptian paintings (see figure 1). Illustrations of butterflies from 3,500 years ago show that they were a familiar part of the surroundings, and they may well have already featured in poetry and mythology. In later Christian teachings the transformation of caterpillars into butterflies was used as a symbol of the Resurrection, and the phenomenon was probably used earlier as a sign of the rebirth of the world in spring. The name butterfly may have been derived from the yellow Brimstone butterfly which appears very early in spring and was called the 'butter coloured fly'. In one rather unexpected and really quite harmless way butterflies also brought a sense of terror to man. The recorded tales of blood raining down from the sky and stains of blood everywhere could have been true in one respect. A drop of red liquid is produced by a butterfly just after it emerges from the chrysalis (see page 38). With the help of a little imagination, the mass emergence of butterflies could produce the 'rain of blood' which was reported.

There is a great deal of evidence that by mediaeval times people were aware of the beauty of butterflies. The illustrated borders of many illuminated manuscripts include butterflies among the other animals and plants (see figure 2). These marginal illustrations, like many later paintings of butterflies, can be divided into three classes. The first comprises the easily identified species which must have been drawn carefully from observations of the living butterfly. These artists may have been the first naturalists intent on making accurate records of flora and fauna. The second class of butterfly illustration is that of insects which resemble some existing species but which are not so carefully drawn: they were probably done from memory on a winter's day! They cannot be positively identified although one can hazard a guess at what the artist had in mind. Finally, there are illustrations where the pattern and colour are clearly from the artist's imagination, being quite unlike any known species.

There is no doubt butterflies had an aesthetic appeal but it is difficult from the early figures and writings to interpret the scholar's view of them apart from that of their transformation, although Albertus Maximus in the thirteenth century suggested that butterflies were 'flying worms'. Later authors tended to deride this but it is an interesting proposal of the idea of a segmented flying animal, and after all, butterflies are derived from a worm-like caterpillar.

By the seventeenth century, books were appearing in Europe which were illustrated with paintings and drawings of animals which included butterflies. Much of the material in different countries was derived from

Figure 2 A typical page from the fourteenth century illuminated manuscript, the St Denis Missal, showing animals and plants in the illustrated border. The pattern of the butterflies resembles that of the Small Tortoiseshell. This would have been a common butterfly around the monastery near Paris where the work was done.

earlier sources, copying some of the fantasy which surrounded the 'unknown' in those days. Throughout Europe new works were appearing and one of the earliest English volumes was *Theatrum Insectorum* (1634) by Thomas Mouffet, who drew on various continental sources as well as his own experience.

The history of the butterflies of Europe, man's awareness of them, and the books written about them, would make a book in itself. By the beginning of the eighteenth century some beautiful works began to appear. The superb illustrations and attention to detail in the drawings in them show that the authors and artists had reared the insects from the caterpillar stage, and had carefully recorded each change. Different species were being collected by travellers and explorers and some, like the famous Maria von Merian who went to South America, sketched the wildlife in its natural surroundings. These people were the forerunners of the explorer-naturalists of later years and they brought back not only their drawings and paintings, but also the insects themselves which formed parts of the huge collections in Paris, Berlin, London and other cities. These collections were used to illustrate books which are now only found in large libraries and museums.

The eighteenth century also saw the development of the cabinet of curios, that strange collection of animal, vegetable and mineral objects which most gentlemen sought to maintain. These collections included butterflies, sometimes pressed between the pages of books, but later pinned on boards. Some of the earliest specimens, collected in about 1680, are still in existence, pressed between pages of books with a flower collection. As books on butterflies were produced so interest in the insects increased. A method of setting and pinning was invented which allowed collectors to display specimens in all their beauty, and collecting became a popular pastime. Detailed accounts of British butterflies and moths began with Petiver's *Papilionum Britanniae* (1717), and continued with new works throughout the century. The illustrations from *The Aurelian* or *Natural History of English Insects* by Moses Harris (1766) (see figure 5) show the technical excellence which was achieved.

Collecting on a grand scale came to a peak in the nineteenth century. Vast sums of money were spent by collectors anxious to obtain new species and to make their collections as complete as possible. Some collectors travelled while others remained at home and employed professional collectors whose lives were frequently at risk as they entered new areas in search of the 'living treasures'. A scientific system of classification had been devised by Carolus Linnaeus in the mid-eighteenth century (see page 39). The nineteenth century was the age of descriptions of new species as is shown in the wealth of books published. These dealt not only with the exotic Lepidoptera under titles like *Sammlung neuer oder wenig bekannter aussereuropaischer Schmetterlinge* by Herrick-Shaffer (1850–58), or *Lepidoptera Exotica* by A.G. Butler (1869–74), but also included works on European butterflies. In most countries authors were busy publishing works on their own fauna. Curtis's *British Entomology* (1823–40) included many butterflies and moths while all the species of British Lepidoptera were figured in colour in Wood's *Index Entomologicus* (1833–39), followed by *British Butterflies and their Transformation* by Westwood and Humphreys (1843). Popular condensed editions, the forerunners of the field guides, appeared, like the *Manual of British Butterflies and Moths* by H.T. Stainton (1856–59), published in monthly parts at threepence an issue. This was followed by the *Handbook of British Lepidoptera* by Edward Meyrick in 1895, a treasured book which is still widely used.

Butterflies and their transformations were popular subjects for children's books in the nineteenth century. Some of the famous children's works, like the *Butterfly Ball and the Grasshopper's Feast* by William Roscoe (1807), were surely written just for entertainment, while others such as those published by the Religious Tracts Society of London had the more definite aim of instructing children in the wonders of nature and the works of God. Several editions were produced, like *The History of Insects* (1839) with a detailed text about insects, and only towards the end of the book is the metamorphosis from caterpillar to butterfly equated with the idea of the Resurrection. *The History of Insects* is a very factual account but Jane Bragg's *Birds and Insects' dialogues in Prose and Verse* (1844) has less technical information and more insistence on the need for kindness and good behaviour towards animals, even insects. Perhaps this is an early example of educating the public in the need for conservation.

A good example of the school prizes awarded at the end of the last century is *Fairy Frisket or Peeps at Insect Life* by A.L.O.E., (A Lady of England, the penname of Charlotte Maria Tucker), (1899). My copy has a note which says it was 'Second prize for Arithmetic, awarded to James Smith, July 1891 by the Merchant Company School, Edinburgh'. All these books stimulated interest in insect life and together with other natural history books led to the popular interest in natural history and the formation of Natural History Societies. The origins and spread of the latter are well documented in David Allen's delightful book *The Naturalist in Britain, a Social History* published by Allen Lane (1976).

Throughout the nineteenth century studies were made on the distribution of butterflies and this, together with work on the various new species being discovered, went on into the twentieth century and is still continuing. Many new species of butterflies are discovered each year, even in Europe where there has been over 200 years of intensive study. For example, two new species of blues (family Lycaenidae) from Greece were described in 1978.

Along with the study of speciation and distribution, other aspects of butterfly natural history have been the centre of attention. Early on many butterflies were bred and the relative ease with which several generations can be produced in the laboratory has led to their use in genetic studies. These studies have been carried on all over the world and have particular

Figure 3 The research work by Professor Sir Cyril Clarke on the inheritance of the Rhesus factor in babies involved the technique of hand-mating Swallowtail butterflies.

importance in medicine. The work carried out by Professor Sir Cyril Clarke and his co-workers on the inheritance of characters in butterflies has led to an understanding of this process in Man. This has enabled the occurence of the potentially lethal Rhesus factor in babies to be predicted, and steps taken to prevent its effect.

Butterfly populations have been studied in an attempt to understand the factors that affect them. These studies, while apparently marginal to our direct use, can lead to an understanding of the effect of different factors on animal populations including Man. The use of butterflies in scientific research is continually being expanded since, far from being just a fringe exercise on some attractive butterfly, it can generate theories and ideas with far reaching implications.

As a hobby, collecting butterflies continues to be popular, and has always contributed much information. Opponents insist that collecting can destroy a rare species and there is little doubt that when the numbers of a species fall below a certain level, excessive collecting of newly emerged individuals could cause further decline of that species. There is, however, little evidence that over-collecting has been responsible for the extinction of any species, although small colonies have been destroyed. In general, the destruction of the environment or a climatic change causes the initial drop in numbers of a species on the edge of its range (see page 66). The collector, could nevertheless deliver the *coup de grâce* when numbers get too low.

Throughout this book I have drawn an analogy between birdwatching and butterfly watching, and I have made suggestions for the butterfly watcher so that he or she may learn more about the habits of butterflies. There are gaps in our knowledge of the behaviour of even the most common butterflies and suggestions are made of how these can be filled by the amateur. You will be surprised how much can be learnt from careful observation, and how much fun can be derived from watching these beautiful insects in their free flying state.

2 Introducing the butterfly

Butterflies in the animal kingdom

Animal and plant life on Earth has been classified into like groups, partly as a result of Man's innate desire to arrange and order his surroundings, but also for the very practical reason of communicating information. Classifications, at least verbal ones, must have started with the earliest hunters – one can imagine the division they made between animals which were good to eat and those which considered Man good to eat! Plants would have been mentally grouped in a similar way into those which could provide food and those which produced illness and perhaps death. Without a classification of the living world no human community could have begun to live together, and even today, subconsciously or consciously, we classify items, whether by price, shape or colour.

There is still no real measure of agreement among zoologists about the classification of the arthropods, the animals with jointed limbs (crabs, millipedes, woodlice, shrimps, spiders and insects). Some arrange them in three distinct groups: the Crustacea, which are the crabs, lobsters and allies, the Chelicerata, the spiders, scorpions, harvestmen and their allies; and the Uniramia, which include myriapods and insects, (see figure 4). Others have a different concept of these groupings. All these animals, from crabs and spiders to myriapods and insects, have certain structures in common. They all have a skeleton, made up of a tough material, outside the body. Unlike Man and other vertebrates, whose skeletal bones are surrounded by flesh, the arthropods have their flesh inside a hard cover or exoskeleton. While this protects the soft parts it has distinct limitations on size and method of growth. The exoskeleton is divided into rings or segments to assist movement. There are several other features that arthropods share, including blood which bathes the organs rather than running in vessels and capillaries and, more obviously, jointed legs.

Now let us consider the main arthropod classes. The Crustacea and their relatives have many legs and their bodies are usually divided into two main regions: the head and thorax fused together (the cephalo-thorax), and the abdomen. They usually have two pairs of antennae-like structures on the head and their appendages, except for the antennae, are mostly double structures. Their respiration is by means of gills or via the body wall. The class is very diverse and includes crabs, barnacles, shrimps and terrestrial woodlice. The Chelicerata includes the spiders, scorpions and ticks. They do not have antennae and most have four pairs of legs.

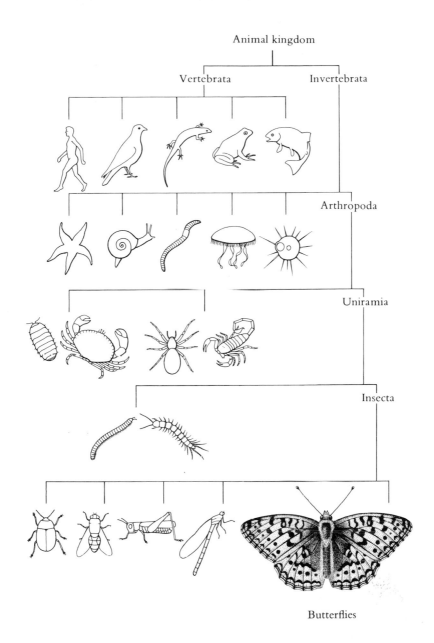

Animal kingdom

Vertebrata   Invertebrata

Arthropoda

Uniramia

Insecta

Butterflies

Figure 4 This simplified representation of the animal kingdom shows the position of butterflies (and moths) in relation to other groups.

Class Uniramia is divided into two groups. In the first of these, the Myriapoda, the centipedes and millipedes have segmented antennae and many legs, one pair only on each segment in centipedes, two pairs on each segment in millipedes. Respiration is by the same system used by insects which is described below. In the second group we come finally to the Insecta, the insects, which include dragonflies, fleas, lice, butterflies, bees, wasps, moths, greenfly and many others. All these insects have the typical arthropod structure mentioned and, in addition and peculiar to insects, possess the following features: body divided into three main parts – head, thorax and abdomen; one pair of antennae; three pairs of legs; and an exoskeleton toughened with a material called chitin.

Insects have respiratory structures called trachea which are tubes running through the body, opening to the air through small holes (spiracles). The aperture of the spiracles can be controlled by the insect and the air partly diffuses, and is partly pumped along by the general body movement to all the organs. There is no active pumping of air into and out of the body (as in the vertebrates), and so respiration is a much slower process and less efficient over long distances. This is another of the constraints limiting the size of insects. Insects have a dorsal blood vessel which acts as a heart pumping the blood round the body, but they have no capillaries as the blood bathes the various tissues. The main divisions of head, thorax and abdomen are further divided into segments, as in most arthropods. This enables the stiff exoskeleton of the insect's body to move rather like the jointed armour of a knight. The segmentation of the head cannot be seen externally; the thorax consists of three segments and the abdomen usually has ten segments. The nervous system of an insect consists of the brain in the head and a series of nerve centres called ganglia, linked by a main nerve trunk running ventrally along the body.

The ability to fly is a characteristic of most insects (all invertebrates that fly are insects but not all insects can fly). Flight originated early in the evolution of insects. Three hundred and fifty million years ago some of the giant dragonflies of the Carboniferous era had wingspans of 600 mm and 300 million years ago many insects existed with well-developed wings. We might pause here to reflect on the ancestry of the butterflies we are so familiar with today. The insects, so fragile in appearance with such short lives, have a very long history. It seems incredible that such ephemeral creatures could have made lasting impressions but quite a number of fossil butterflies are known. It is exciting to imagine butterflies flitting around the heads of the last of the dinosaurs millions of years ago and others, later, attracting the attention of prehistoric Man.

Figure 5 One of the famous early English butterfly books is *The Aurelian or Natural History of English Insects, namely butterflies and moths together with the plants on which they feed*, by Moses Harris. It was first published in 1766 and has superb, technically accurate illustrations of the insects and the foodplants of the caterpillars. This photograph is reproduced from the original colour paintings by Moses Harris in the library of the British Museum (Natural History).

PAINTED LADY See Linn: Cardui 197
a the Catt.r b. the Chrysalis. c the Fly. d the Underside
Catt: feeds on thistles in June, change into Chrys:
in July and the fly appears in Aug:t

MARMORIS. Linn: Pag: Galathea. 147.
e Cat.r feeds on grass in the spring, Changes to Chry: f.
in May and the fly the beginning of June. g.
h. the underside the Male; and i. the Under of female

Mo.s Harris pinx.

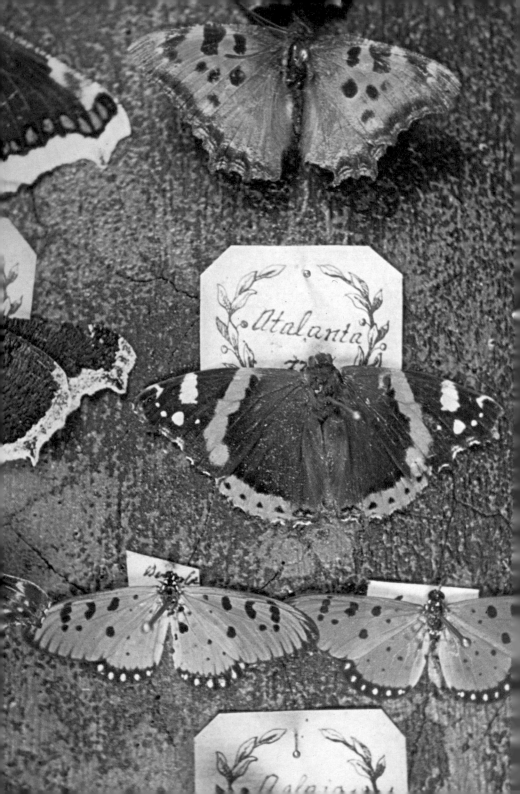

Atalanta

Flight is vital to many insects for dispersal, mate seeking and escape from predators, and the wings themselves form colourful displays and protection devices (see page 103), act as heat exchangers (see page 24) and assist gaseous exchange by acting as an aerial gill.

When you watch insects it is soon apparent that they fly in different ways. Butterflies have a mechanism which couples together the fore- and hindwings enabling them to work in unison and evidently more efficiently (see figure 7). This is caused by the amount of overlap of a slightly enlarged area of hindwing, the humeral lobe. Some butterflies, like the Scarce Swallowtail and the Swallowtail, are good at gliding while others, like the Peacock and Large or Cabbage White, glide only briefly. Studies have been made on the mechanism of insect flight using wind tunnels and high-speed photography. Although the wings may look as though they flap up and down, photography has shown that the

Figure 7 A high-speed flash photograph shows a Green-veined White butterfly in flight with the fore- and hindwings overlapping and coupled together.

tips of the wings perform a near figure of eight. The wings are moved by muscles anchored in the rigid thorax. If the thorax in cross-section is considered as a box with a lid which fits inside it, as the lid is moved down by indirect muscles, so the wings, inserted between lid and the box, move upwards. The down-stroke of the wings is aided by muscles which work from the front to the back of the box, pulling it back into shape and thus moving the lid upwards. The control of the flight, especially at take-off,

Figure 6 The collection of Clerck, an eighteenth century naturalist, contains specimens on which Linnaeus based many of his descriptions of species. The butterflies and their decorative labels were kept in specially lined drawers. A Large Tortoiseshell can be seen at the top and a Red Admiral in the centre. Below are two specimens of *Acraea violae* from India. The wingtips of a Camberwell Beauty are clearly recognisable in the left margin. The Clerck Collection is housed in Stockholm.

is highly developed and the landing is an instant stop, a remarkable deceleration which must exert a tremendous strain on the insect structure.

There are some twenty-three main insect groups or Orders and, although the exact number varies according to the classification used, each Order is characterised in different ways. Beetles (Order Coleoptera) have hardened forewings (elytra), flies (Order Diptera), like the common housefly or the mosquito, have only one pair of wings. Wasps (Order Hymenoptera) have two pairs of wings and the particular arrangement of the veins in the wings distinguishes them from other insects. The differences between dragonflies and greenfly are obvious (Orders Odonata and Hemiptera) but it is less easy to tell at a glance a dragonfly from an ant-lion (Orders Odonata and Neuroptera). The scaly-winged insects or Lepidoptera, the butterflies and moths, are fortunately quite easy to recognise. However, even here some are surprisingly different with various moths skilfully disguising themselves to look like wasps.

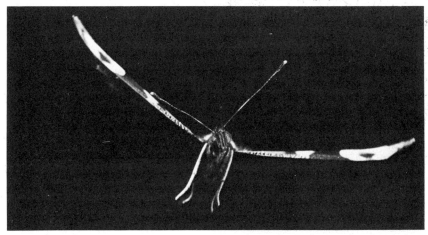

Figure 8 An unusual head-on view of a Peacock butterfly in flight. Notice the slightly upturned apex of the wings as the figure of eight movement is performed by the tips. This is a high-speed flash photograph.

Butterfly structure

Butterflies and moths have all the general characteristics of the arthropods and the insects together with some specialities. These include the overlapping rows of scales on the wings (see figure 11) which rub off as powder. These scales carry the colour pigments and their arrangement forms the complicated wing patterns we see. Special scales also act as scent dispersants and release pheromones, chemicals which enable the butterfly or moth to recognise its mate or to mark its territory (see page 96).

The antennae on the head carry many microscopic sense organs for detecting events in the insect's surroundings. There is a pair of large compound eyes, one on either side of the head. Each eye is made up of many separate facets or ommatidea, each of which sends messages to the brain. As you approach a butterfly your image or shadow will stimulate thousands of these separate ommatidea, and your movement will be quickly detected. These eyes not only perceive movement but also detect light and dark as well as colour. Many butterflies also have simple eyes or ocelli on top of the head. These may also detect changes in the intensity of light but are believed not to form images. Butterflies and moths are attracted to flowers by colour as well as by scent. Recent studies have shown that red, orange and yellow colours in butterflies, especially in the families Nymphalidae and Pieridae, are not just associated with warning coloration. Butterflies have the broadest visible spectrum of any animal, ranging from the ultra-violet at one end to yellow-orange and red at the other. Recognition of these colours by the butterflies means that they are used not only for protection (see page 81)

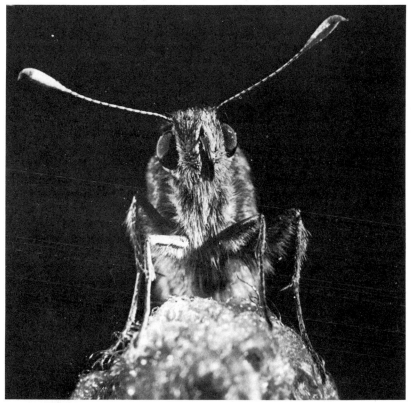

Figure 9 This head-on view of a butterfly shows several characteristic features. The club-ended antennae, large compound eyes and central proboscis curled up below the head are clearly seen. Long scales cover the whole of the body and head and the jointed legs with spines are also visible.

but also for communication. The red and orange and yellows can be seen and the pattern and arrangements of the colours conveys information within or perhaps between species.

Additional sensory structures, the palps, are found below the head in the Lepidoptera. There may be one or two pairs of these in moths but there is only one pair in butterflies. Between the palps arises the tongue or proboscis, a structure unique to the Lepidoptera. Many other insects have sucking mouthparts (greenfly, mosquitoes, bugs, for example) but none can coil them up like a watch spring under the head, to be uncoiled and extended when needed for feeding. Recent observations on an American butterfly suggest that the proboscis may serve other minor functions. In these observations a skipper butterfly was seen using its

Figure 10 Butterflies and moths are the only insects which can coil the proboscis when it is not in use. This enables them to have a much longer feeding apparatus to reach deep into flowers for nectar. This is a Peacock about to feed on Buddleia.

proboscis to remove water droplets from its wings and to insert the proboscis between its scales. Could it have been preening?

Under its heavy covering of scales the thorax is divided into three main segments. All three have a pair of legs on the ventral surface and the rear two segments, the meso- and meta-thorax, also carry a pair of wings each. The wings are flat, but can be considered as two layers through which run the series of very distinct veins, sometimes called nerves or nervules. The arrangement of these veins is more or less constant within a species and is characteristic for the species. Species with similar venation are placed in the same family. The veins enable the wing to be fully expanded when the crumpled butterfly or moth first emerges from the chrysalis or pupa. Liquid called haemolymph, which is the insect's blood, is forced along them and the wings spread out. It was once believed that the wings were dead structures, but we now realise that even in the fully expanded wings circulation of blood from the body still continues. The veins and some of the spaces between them have been given names to make comparison between species easier. There is usually a difference in the pattern and colours between the upper and lower sides of the wings and between the fore- and hindwings.

Wing and body scales in butterflies and moths are of many different shapes and resemble flattened bags inserted in a socket, and arranged in rows overlapping one another, especially on the wings. The scales not only provide colour and pattern but are also important in flight; if too many are rubbed off the butterfly can scarcely fly. Some are modified for scent dispersal and are often arranged in rows or groups (see figure 9). In some of the skipper butterflies the scales arranged in line along a vein are black while most of the other wing scales are a reddish orange. These black scales form the sex or scent brand in the male and enable it to be distinguished from the female quite readily. They also play an important part in the sex recognition for the butterflies themselves during courtship (see page 96). Sex brands can also help us to distinguish the males of two very similar species, the Essex Skipper and the Small Skipper. In the latter the male has a distinctive black line along the veins of the upperside in the middle of the forewing, while in the Essex Skipper there are very few black scales and the sex brand is not conspicuous.

The constancy of pattern and colour in the wings of butterflies and moths is primarily determined by the genetic makeup of the individual. Sometimes this goes wrong and instead of normal fore- and hindwing patterns, some of the forewing pattern may appear on the hindwings and vice versa. Genetic effects may also sometimes produce a male pattern on the fore- and hindwings on one side of the body, while the wings on the other side carry the female pattern. These individuals, gynandromorphs, are rare and in fact the incredible constancy of pattern and colour in many individuals and over many generations is a remarkable feature of butterflies.

Apart from the functions already mentioned scale colours play a part

Figure 11 This enlarged photograph of the wing scales of a Grayling butterfly shows the overlapping arrangement and the tufts of the smaller scent scales.

in the temperature control of butterflies. The butterfly's body temperature fluctuates according to the outside temperature and so ways of warming up are important. Many butterflies spread their wings to receive the full effect of sunlight, and the darker pigments of the scales absorb more of the heat than the lighter ones. This raises the temperature of the blood passing through the veins in the wings, which also increases the overall temperature as it circulates around the rest of the body. Even when the air temperature is relatively low sunlight will warm up the butterfly sufficiently for it to fly, a very useful device on a cool spring morning. This feature characterises butterflies as heliotherms, contrasting with many moths which are myotherms. Night-flying moths have to warm up in the absence of sunlight and can often be seen vibrating their wings, increasing their body temperature by muscular activity. The wing scales may also act like the insulating fur of a mammal, for once the body of the moth or butterfly is warm enough for flight, the air trapped between the scales will stop excessive heat loss. Butterflies may also disperse some of the heat they have built up by resting in the shade with their wings open, when heat loss through the thin wings can easily occur. Wings and scales have therefore many functions, apart from colour and flight.

The three pairs of legs on the thorax of a butterfly are jointed and consist of an apical claw or claws, usually five short tarsal segments, and a thicker and longer tibia articulating with the femur. This then attaches by another two smaller parts to the body. The legs carry a number of spines.

The abdomen usually consists of ten segments, without any appendages in the Lepidoptera, although some moths have a structure connected with reception of sound at the base of the abdomen. Inside the tip of the abdomen of the male are the chitinised structures of the reproductive organs or genitalia. These are everted during mating and used to grasp the tip of the female's abdomen. The genitalia are studied in the classification of the Lepidoptera, but can only be properly seen when they are removed from the dead insect and put on a slide for examination through a microscope.

Butterflies and moths

There are some 165,000 species of Lepidoptera arranged in 120 to 150 families (depending upon the classification used) of which 15,000 are butterflies in only eight families; the rest are moths. The butterfly families are sometimes called the Rhopalocera and the moth families the Heterocera. It is usually quite easy to recognise the differences between butterflies and moths (see figure 12) but these are more difficult to characterise biologically. Most butterflies fly by day and moths fly by night. Butterflies generally have antennae with clubbed or swollen tips, whereas the antennae of moths are thin, or perhaps very pectinate (feathery), never seen in butterflies. Moths tend to have fat, furry-looking bodies, while butterflies have a slight waist between thorax and abdomen, and there are differences in the wing venation and in the wing-coupling mechanism. Butterflies often (but not always) sit with their wings spread while a few moths sit in this way as well. The difficulty in identifying differences between butterflies and moths lies in their close relationship; butterflies are merely one small group of families in the Order Lepidoptera.

Moths have diverged in shape and habits far more than butterflies which, by comparison, are a rather conservative group. There are many day-flying moths like the burnets, but the vast majority fly at night. The wing shapes of moths are more varied than those of butterflies and some can rival butterflies with their colours although most are less vivid. After all, flying by night when colour and pattern cannot be seen, and resting by day, calls for coloration to camouflage the moth from diurnal predators rather than advertise presence. Although many species of butterflies have modified the outlines of their wings, and some have tails, none demonstrate the extremes of some moths in the family Zygaenidae, whose hindwings are each reduced to a narrow streamer. Some species of moths have wingless females, a phenomenon which does not occur in butterflies. Many butterflies are well camouflaged but none try to look like wasps or bees, a form of mimicry used by moths.

The range of food on which the caterpillars of moths feed is much wider than that of butterfly caterpillars, and the overall size range of the adults,

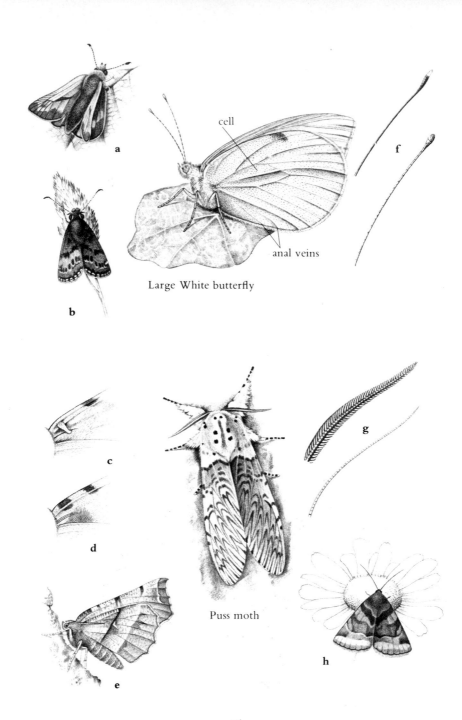

a

b

cell

anal veins

Large White butterfly

f

c

d

g

e

Puss moth

h

from a few millimetres to over 300 millimetres wingspan, is much greater. Many more species of moths are pests of agriculture, horticulture and forestry, not forgetting the pests of stored food and clothes. It is pleasant to be able to say that butterflies are far less of a problem to Man.

The life-histories of butterflies and moths are broadly similar. The four stages of the life-cycle are well defined and contrast with those of some other insects like grasshoppers. In the latter the egg hatches into a small grasshopper-like insect which lacks wings and is not sexually mature. This grows, getting larger in stages by moulting with the wings increasing in size but not functional, until the last stage moults into the adult insect. This is often called the imago and it is winged and sexually mature. In the Lepidoptera the egg hatches into a caterpillar, and this later becomes a chrysalis or pupa from which the adult flying insect emerges. The young stages are thus totally different in appearance from the adult, and the term 'complete metamorphosis' is used for this dramatic change of shape.

The life of a butterfly

Butterfly eggs vary in shape according to the species. Under a lens or microscope they appear as objects of beauty with much detailed sculpturing. The eggs of the swallowtails are spherical, slightly flattened and ribbed, but these ribs are not as conspicuous as they are on the eggs of other species. The eggs of skippers are very variable in shape, some being globular and ribbed, others flattened and broader than tall. The eggs of the whites are ribbed and rather bottle shaped while those of the satyrids and nymphalids are globular, often flattened at the top. Those of the White Admiral are very distinctive with a complicated raised reticulate pattern, and a small spine on each hexagonal piece (see figure 14). The lycaenids have a flattened egg with a complicated pattern. In many cases the eggs hatch in about a week, but overwintering eggs may not hatch for six months. The tiny larva formed inside bites its way through the eggshell and emerges as a perfect caterpillar. Many caterpillars first eat the shell of the egg from which they have hatched before starting to feed on their hostplant.

A caterpillar is tube-like and consists of a head followed by thirteen segments. There are two distinct types in the butterflies: the cylindrical, worm-like, and woodlouse or slug-like. The head with its shiny chitin gives an impression of huge eyes, like those of the adult, but in fact

Figure 12 Some of the differences between butterflies and moths. The Large White butterfly and Puss moth are shown in typical resting positions. As exceptions, the Large Skipper (**a**) rests with wings at different angles; the Dingy Skipper (**b**) rests in a moth-like position; the Early Thorn moth rests in a butterfly-like position (**e**); and the colourful Burnet Companion moth (**h**) flies during the day and at rest resembles a skipper. The antennae of butterflies are typically clubbed (**f**), while those of moths are feathery or thin (**g**). The wing-coupling mechanism of moths is more complicated than the simple overlapping of fore- and hindwing in butterflies, and differs between males (**c**) and females (**d**).

The ribbed egg is attached to Garlic Mustard,
one of the foodplants of the caterpillar

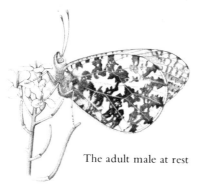

The adult male at rest

Both the caterpillar and chrysalis
are well camouflaged on the plant

Figure 13 The four stages in the life-cycle of a butterfly, in this case an Orange Tip.

Figure 14 The single egg of a White Admiral (left) laid on the upperside of a Honeysuckle leaf contrasts with the round, smooth eggs of the Speckled Wood (right) on a grass leaf.

caterpillars have a group of small eyespots, called ocelli, towards the bottom of the head (see figure 15). Like those in the adult, it is thought that these are merely light sensitive organs with little function of image formation. By moving its head from side to side the caterpillar is able to produce an impression of shapes and to detect movement.

Below the head are the mandibles which are well developed for chewing food, minute antennae and, centrally placed, a short process called the spinneret, from which silk is produced. On each of the three segments following the head, corresponding to the thorax of the adult, is a pair of

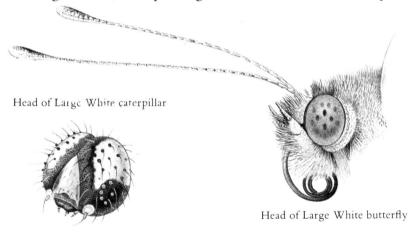

Head of Large White caterpillar

Head of Large White butterfly

Figure 15 At first glance the large, glossy areas on the caterpillar's head could be mistaken for enormous eyes but they are merely part of the head capsule. The six simple eyes (ocelli) are arranged in a circle on each side, and the jaws are concealed below the head. The butterfly head shows the long, curled proboscis, large compound eyes and long antennae (see also figure 9).

short legs with claws. Towards the middle of the body the sixth, seventh, eighth and ninth segments carry a pair of prolegs, short stump-like legs with a circlet of tiny hooks at their tips. Then there are two more segments without legs, and at the very top of the abdomen a pair of legs called claspers. A series of small holes called spiracles runs along each side of the caterpillar, from which the trachea or breathing tubes run through the body. The slug-like caterpillars have small heads which can be withdrawn into the first segment. The body of the caterpillar is often covered with hairs, sometimes branched, and spines.

Internally, the caterpillar has a digestive tract running from the mouth to the anus at the tip of the abdomen. The waste food is expelled through the anus as small hard pellets called frass. This is often mistaken for eggs but of course it is only the adult butterflies, not the caterpillars, that can lay eggs. The caterpillar can be considered merely as a feeding and growing tube. Like the adult insect the caterpillar has an exoskeleton surrounding its body and the muscles are attached to the tough body wall, rather like the way in which the muscles of a mammal are attached to its bones.

The segmentation of the caterpillar gives it mobility but to grow larger it has to moult its rigid skin. This is done by the caterpillar first growing a new skin below the old; the old skin splits and the caterpillar struggles out rather like a finger being withdrawn from a glove. It swallows air and this expands and stretches the body before the new exoskeleton hardens. The caterpillar repeats this process several times, getting larger each time. The process of skin changing is called moulting, and each stage between moults is called an instar. There are usually four moults and the number is always constant within the species. The outer skin is shed as well as the chitinised linings of part of the trachea, and

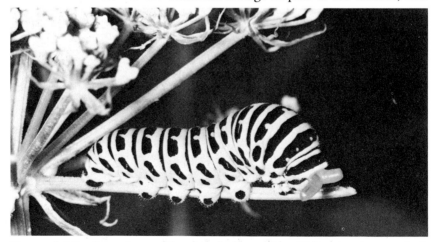

Figure 16 A Swallowtail caterpillar everts the osmaterium. This orange-brown tube is normally concealed within the body and everted when the caterpillar is threatened.

other parts formed from the exoskeleton. Moulting is a very complicated procedure and the caterpillar is particularly vulnerable at this time. It generally spins a small platform of silk on a twig or leaf to which it fastens itself while undergoing a moult.

It is obviously important that the vulnerable non-flying caterpillar is protected as well as possible to ensure it can carry out its prime function – the subsequent production of the adult. One way this is achieved is by overproduction. Far more eggs are laid than will ever survive, and far more first instar caterpillars hatch from the eggs than survive to the second instar. Therefore, although the number of caterpillars diminishes through the instars, the system ensures that enough adults are produced for the population to survive.

Butterfly eggs are often parasitised. Small wasp-like insects may lay their eggs inside the butterfly eggs, and the wasp grub develops in the food that was meant for the young caterpillar. Eggs are frequently eaten by other insects, and bugs of the Order Hemiptera may suck the contents with their proboscis. Studies on the numbers of eggs laid and the losses by various causes would be an interesting project for a student. Most loss occurs during the caterpillar stage; this is the longest stage of the life-cycle so there is more time for caterpillars to be discovered by parasites and predators, which are also attracted by their increasing size.

Survival methods in caterpillars are just as complex as those of the adult butterflies discussed in chapter five. Swallowtail caterpillars, for example, evert a forked process called the osmaterium, from behind the head (see figure 16). This has an unpleasant smell to emphasise the

Figure 17 The gregarious spiny caterpillars of the Small Tortoiseshell spin a web of silk under which they all live.

unpalatable nature of the caterpillar. Small Tortoiseshell larvae live in groups in a web on the leaves of Nettle (see figure 17). Apart from the concealment provided by the web they also have protection from the spines all over their bodies, and also perhaps from the Nettles on which they live. Many caterpillars are colourful and distasteful. Those of the Monarch, feeding on a plant which is poisonous to other animals, utilise the poisons in the food to give themselves protection. Other caterpillars feeding on distasteful plants also utilise plant chemicals for their own defence.

Caterpillars which are basically tubular in shape would be very conspicuous on flat leaves, and so many have adopted a special counter-shading. With a dark back facing the light and a paler colour underneath the body, they tend to be less obvious to a predatory eye. Camouflage is an obvious method of avoiding detection and many caterpillars of the browns, for example, adopt concealment colours when feeding on grass.

A few species adopt a more active defence. The caterpillars of the Large or Cabbage White feed gregariously on our garden Cabbage, and they start and stop feeding in unison as if in response to a signal. Perhaps the combined action of a number of individuals gives the impression of a large unit (like a well-drilled army)? These caterpillars have an unpleasant smell and are probably also distasteful to some birds. Fortunately for us Large White caterpillars also have enemies in the form of tiny parasitic wasps, for we might otherwise find our plants completely destroyed by them. Some caterpillars of the fritillaries, like the Heath Fritillary, for example, also have an active protection habit and if alarmed throw up their heads together.

Figure 18 The caterpillar of the Purple Emperor is green with pale yellow stripes and so it is perfectly camouflaged on the leaf.

Figure 19 These newly hatched caterpillars of the Large White are being attacked by a parasitic wasp, *Apanteles*, which lays its eggs inside their bodies. The wasp larvae develop inside and eventually kill the caterpillars.

Skipper caterpillars live in tubes which they make by curling up grass blades. When they produce frass it is thrown clear of the tube by a special structure on the abdomen. Accumulations of frass might make the otherwise inconspicuous roll of grass more obvious, and attract the unwelcome attention of birds looking for a meal. A few species, like the Silver-washed Fritillary caterpillars, curl themselves up into a ring if they are disturbed. They roll to the ground and lie quite still, playing 'possum'.

The wasps which parasitise Large White caterpillars have just been mentioned; in fact there are several species of both small wasp-like insects (Order Hymenoptera) and true flies (Order Diptera) which kill caterpillars in this way. The parasite lays its eggs in or on the caterpillar and the resulting larvae feed on their host, eventually destroying it. The most frequently seen example is that of the Large White. When the parasitised caterpillar is ready to pupate it crawls off the plant and on to a

Figure 20 A Large White caterpillar surrounded by the cocoons of the parasitic wasp larvae that have emerged from its body.

wall or fence. (The example Richard Lewington has drawn in figure 20 was in fact one of the many discovered in his front porch.) Many small larvae then burst out from inside the caterpillar and it never actually pupates. Each larva spins a cocoon of golden yellow silk and the result is a mass of these around the dried-out caterpillars. Do not destroy the cocoons for this is the next generation of insects which will control the caterpillars feeding on your Cabbage!

A local increase in the number of parasites can reduce the butterfly population considerably. Parasites kill individual caterpillars but if they are too successful they too will soon die out. There is a balance in nature which tends to prevent this. The term 'balance' although widely used, is perhaps the wrong word since it suggests a steady state which does not occur in the natural world. 'Pendulum' is a better word, indicating the

Figure 21 The Large Blue caterpillar completes its development inside an ants' nest. In this photograph the caterpillar is rearing up just prior to being carried off by the ant. A description of the amazing life-cycle of this species is given in Appendix 1.

continual swing between abundance and scarcity of the various inter-acting species. However, the term pendulum implies an even swing which is probably still not an accurate reflection of events. The pendulum of nature is a feature of all stages of the butterfly population and its survival, but in many cases Man, as a part of nature, has altered the balance and certainly upset the delicate swing of the pendulum. The methods caterpillars adopt to stay alive make very interesting study, and indeed, information on factors controlling the size of an insect popula-tion is of great importance to an entomologist studying pest species.

The change of metamorphosis from the earth-bound caterpillar to the winged butterfly is a remarkable event in nature. Metamorphosis occurs

Figure 22 The Heath Fritillary is a species whose pattern can be very variable and these two photographs show the typical form (above) and an extreme aberration (below). Differences can also extend to the pattern of the upperside. This kind of variation occurs in only a small percentage of the population of a species.

in the fifth instar after the fourth moult when the caterpillar is fully grown. The caterpillar's whole behaviour changes; instead of looking for food it now moves off to a place of safety for the transformation to a chrysalis to take place. At this time it becomes immobile, and although this is called the resting stage, tremendous changes are taking place inside. We might wonder why the caterpillar does not just grow wings and fly away rather like the young of the more primitive grass-hoppers? The answer lies in the advantage of increasing the exploitation of the environment during the life-cycle. The young nymphs and adult grasshoppers live in very similar ways, feeding more or less on the same plants. The two stages in the life-cycle of butterflies and other insects (bees, wasps, ants, beetles, flies) enable these insects to specialise in feeding in two distinct ways. The larva or caterpillar can be highly adapted for one way of life while the aerial adult stage is adapted and specialised for a totally different way of life. No compromise is necessary and the ability

Figure 25 Some butterfly chrysalids. The Small Tortoiseshell is attached by hooks (the cremaster) at the base and hangs free. The moulted skin of the caterpillar is still attached. The Holly Blue is attached at the tip of the abdomen but is also secured by a girdle of silk. The Marbled White caterpillar pupates on the ground where the chrysalid lies hidden.

to exploit two often very different habitats in one life-cycle affords great potential for the development of specialised forms. The largest number of species now living occur in the insect Orders which have a complete metamorphosis in their life-cycle.

Having settled down in its resting stage the caterpillar again sheds its skin but this time, instead of another caterpillar appearing, the chrysalis is formed. The outer covering hardens and the next phase is ready to begin. There are many different shapes of chrysalids and many different sites are selected to conceal them. There are no external moveable appendages on the chrysalis although it can wriggle a little, and many are angular with processes (see figure 25). The chrysalis is often well

Figure 24 The Purple Emperor is a woodland species which feeds high up in the tree-tops. The males are readily attracted to damp patches of earth and to carrion, dung and urine-soaked earth, but the females remain in the tree-tops. The upperside of the male is an iridescent purple.

camouflaged although many have bright reflective colours (the gold spot on some chrysalids was called an Aurelius, and gave rise to the name Aurelians for early butterfly collectors). The chrysalis does not feed or move from the spot to which it is anchored. Each species has its own particular methods of attachment. Some chrysalids hang downwards, usually with a girdle of silk around them, while others are fixed so that the free end points upwards, again with the silk girdle. A chrysalis is anchored to the basal pad by a group of hooks, the cremaster, at the pointed (abdominal) end.

What happens while the insect is in the chrysalis stage? Those features of the caterpillar which will not be needed by the adult are dissolved, and the energy and material released help to build the adult structures. Most of the adult features are present in the caterpillar as groups of unspecialised cells, and these form the new organs by dividing, multiplying and being organised under chemical (hormonal) control from glands near the brain. It has been shown that when these glands are removed from the caterpillar it will not change into a chrysalis. Some of the adult structures, the proboscis and antennae, for example, can usually be seen through the chrysalis skin, and later, just prior to emergence, some of the wing colour shows through. The great day finally arrives and the winged butterfly begins to emerge from the chrysalis. The skin splits along the back and the butterfly pushes its way out appearing not as the glossy final product, but as a crumpled apology of a butterfly with wings folded and wrinkled. It sits still for a time while the blood is gradually forced into the wings through the veins, causing the wing membrane to expand into a 'flat balloon'. The internal strands connecting the upper and lower surfaces stop the wing swelling into a 'round balloon'. Once fully expanded the wings are held out for a while to dry before being brought together. Just as this happens, or a little before, the butterfly squeezes a drop of reddish fluid composed of the stored up excretory products of the chrysalis stage, from its anus. The time from emergence to fully expanded and dry wings can be up to two hours or more in large butterflies, but is much shorter in small ones. Once the wings are dry the butterfly generally feels the need to feed and flies to the nearest flower to drink its nectar.

The whole cycle, from egg to adult, is the life of a butterfly. In most cases the growing, moulting and chrysalis stage is far longer than the adult butterfly stage (contrasting, for example, with Man). A few butterflies which hibernate over winter may live for six to ten months, but the lives of adult butterflies are generally much shorter than this. This has been a brief, general account of the butterfly life-cycle. If you are interested in how life-cycles of individual species differ, there is an Appendix provided with more notes on the life histories of common European species.

3 Butterfly names

Here is a list of butterfly names: Le Morio, Trauermantel, Sorgmantel, Antiope, Camberwell Beauty and Mourning Cloak. These may sound like different species of butterflies but they are in fact just a few of the names used in different countries for the same species. In Britain alone the same butterfly has been known over the years as the Willow Beauty, White Petticoat and the White-bordered Butterfly. The confusion that can arise from the multiplicity of names, and the difficulties that can be caused in identification in these circumstances, can easily be imagined. The solution is simple: one name for each species should be used throughout the world so that scientists, naturalists and all others interested, can be certain that they are referring to the same insect; or indeed to the same plant or animal, for the problem of common names is the same throughout the natural world. But which name should be accepted for international use?

Up to the eighteenth century newly identified plants or animals were given a descriptive sentence which could run to several lines: one can imagine a naturalist saying 'Look at that white butterfly with the two black spots on the forewing and black tips to the wing', by which time the butterfly would have flown away! As correspondence increased between naturalists, the difficulty of communicating information about particular species increased. Vernacular names differed not only between countries but also between different areas of the same country.

Our present method of classification began with the great Swedish naturalist Carolus Linnaeus (1707–1778). His system was based on natural characters which grouped organisms with similar structures together. Having devised his classification, his greatest single contribution to clearing the confusion of names was 'binomial nomenclature', the use of two-word latinized names for plants and animals. Similar animals were grouped together under one (generic) name. For example, Linnaeus put the various species of cats into the genus *Felis* and then gave each species a different name: *Felis leo* is the Lion; *Felis tigris* the Tiger and *Felis onca* the Jaguar. The name he used for butterflies was *Papilio*: *Papilio machaon* was his name for the Swallowtail and *Papilio brassicae* the Large or Cabbage White. He also subdivided his generic groups but the main principle was binomial, that is two names for each species. Linnaeus used this system for all the animals and plants known in his day and his system gradually became accepted as people learnt how to use his classification. When a new species of cat *Felis*, or butterfly *Papilio*, not already in Linnaeus' encyclopaedic *Systema Naturae*, was discovered, naturalists set to and described it. They used the generic name chosen by Linnaeus to convey the general features of the animal, and then gave it a new specific name and explained how it differed from the existing named species.

From Linnaeus, and his works *Species Plantarum* (1753) and *Systema Naturae* (1758), the botanists and zoologists thus started their nomenclature. Over the years many more species and genera were discovered and named. It was almost inevitable that, as naturalists found more and more new species, chaos would once again creep into the system. Two naturalists would independently publish descriptions of the same animal, each one convinced that his was the first description of that species. A great many errors were made because of the difficulty of describing animals accurately, especially insects, whose individuality might depend on whether the wings were described as blue-green or greenish-blue, or whether they had two or three spots on the margins. Colours, especially of insects, are quite difficult to describe so that others can understand and recognise the species.

After a series of shaky starts a measure of international agreement was reached and a code of practice drawn up in 1842. This finally became (for animals) the *International Code of Zoological Nomenclature* and its cornerstone was priority. The name to be used was the earliest published and this basic principle was intended to resolve any confusion. Unfortunately agreement was not always reached on the date of the earliest description, or on the need to change a long-established name for an older, but unused one. To administer the code an august international body of scientists, the Commissioners of Zoological Nomenclature, now adjudicate on controversies and publish their deliberations in the multivolume *Bulletin of Zoological Nomenclature*.

This may seem to be a considerable amount of effort just to establish a stable scientific name. Why do we bother? The confusion of multiple names and the use of the wrong one could lead to a health-hazard, crop loss in agriculture and problems in environmental studies. Consider pest control, a 'multimillion dollar' industry. Control of an insect in one continent may be achieved in a particular way. Let us suppose that a similar insect is also a pest in another continent. If this insect has been misidentified and given the name of that in the published account of the control measure, the method of control may be used again and fail completely. So, if you are to communicate the correct information about a situation, you must not only recognise the species, which is a problem of identification, but you must also use the correct name, a problem of nomenclature. It is therefore important to adopt the same scientific name for a particular animal all over the world; in reality the classification of animals and plants also becomes used as an international language.

The scientific name of the insect we started with, Le Morio, Camberwell Beauty and so on, is *Nymphalis antiopa*, and it is by this name that it is internationally known. The generic name, which always starts with a capital letter, is *Nymphalis* and the specific name, which always starts with a lower case (small) letter, is *antiopa*. The generic name *Nymphalis* will always be applied to butterflies with major characters similar to those of *Nymphalis antiopa*, as for instance in the Large Tortoiseshell *Nymphalis polychloros*. The different specific name, however, shows that there are specific differences between them. Now note the danger of comparing common names. The common name Large Tortoiseshell is very similar to the common name Small Tortoiseshell, but they are not in fact related as can be seen from the scientific name of the Small Tortoiseshell, *Aglais urticae*. A further name is frequently added after the scientific one. This may well be an abbreviation and is the name of the person who first described the species. For example, *Nymphalis antiopa* L. or *N. antiopa* Linn., signifies that this butterfly was first described by Linnaeus.

In the classification of the animal kingdom each group is made up of a number of similar and related animals (see figure 4). For example:

Kingdom	Animalia	animals not plants
Phylum	Arthropoda	animals with jointed legs with outside skeleton; for example, crabs, lobsters, spiders and insects
Class	Insecta	six-legged arthropods with body divided into head, throax and abdomen; for example, beetles, wasps, flies and butterflies
Order	Lepidoptera	scaly-winged insects (butterflies and moths)

How is a butterfly given a scientific name? If a *Papilio* butterfly is discovered which cannot be matched with any of the existing described species then it may well be new to science. Once several specimens of the butterfly have been studied, a publication is prepared giving a description of the new species and showing the differences between it and existing species which already have scientific names. One of the specimens on which the description is based is designated the 'holotype'. Once the description is published the species is then known by the name given. Should any dispute on the concept of the species arise in the future because more specimens have been discovered, it is the holotype specimen, the name-bearer, that is re-examined to confirm the correct identity of the species. It is unfortunate that by its very nature, a *species* cannot really be described definitely: species consists of tens of thousands (or millions) of individuals. The description on which the concept of the species is decided is usually based on a few specimens, and from this the scientist says what he *thinks* the species is. Many disputes inevitably arise about the definitions and delineations of a species. In Britain vernacular or popular names are well established for all species and so you can safely refer to the Camberwell Beauty. If you talk to someone from another country, however, it is better to refer to *Nymphalis antiopa*, to ensure that you both know which species is under discussion.

Further names which may be encountered in books on butterflies are subspecies, and varieties or aberrations. Subspecies are names, usually scientific, given to *populations* of a species with slight differences in pattern, or in the time of emergence (see page 107) from the more typical ones. They are usually geographically isolated. Variations (vars) and aberrations (abs) are *individuals* which differ slightly from the rest of the population (see figure 22). They are usually rare in the population and are much sought after by collectors.

The butterfly families

Grouping similar objects into larger units is a natural shorthand technique to facilitate discussion. However, in these groups of fairly natural units the species are arranged by us into genera, and then these genera into families. Families and genera are man-made concepts and, while in a natural classification they have some meaning, they are nevertheless open to differing interpretations. To some extent this is also true of species, but it is in the generic and sometimes the family classification that most disagreement about the groups in a classification arises. This explains some of the differing scientific names and slightly different families used in other works. These arise because of the subjective nature of the decisions made when entomologists classify insects. Entomologists who are 'splitters' look for small differences and tend to use more family and generic names and have fewer units in each group. The 'lumpers', on the other hand, look at overall similarities and tend to place the species in larger units with families containing many genera, and genera with many included species.

A good example can occur in the family Nymphalidae (see below) which contains many species including the tortoiseshells, peacocks and fritillaries. Some entomologists also include the browns (family Satyridae), but put them in the division below a family creating the subfamily Satyrinae of the Nymphalidae, and reducing the tortoiseshell, peacock and fritillary groups to subfamilies. Here I follow those who regard these divisions as separate families and will therefore refer to the browns of the family Satyridae, and the peacocks of the family Nymphalidae. In all cases family names end in -idae and subfamily names in -inae. (This is true of all family and subfamily names in the animal kingdom.)

The genus, which contains a number of similar species, produces even more disagreement among entomologists. When looking at differences between species some people take a more restricted view and have many genera, while others looking at broad similarities may group many species together in one genus. In the fritillaries there are examples where different generic names have been used. Most of the fritillaries were formerly placed in the genus *Argynnis*. Further studies gradually showed that the species in this genus were not as closely related as first thought, and so they were separated into at least thirteen different generic names. In some recent works many of these have been ignored and *Argynnis* used again for the majority of the fritillaries. The classification adopted depends on the generic concept of the writer, and it is important to be aware of this problem when looking through the literature. The following list is of the generic names currently used for species of European fritillaries:

Argynnis	*Euphydryas*	*Mesoacidalia*
Argyronome	*Eurodryas*	*Pandoriana*
Brenthis	*Issoria*	*Proclossiana*
Boloria	*Melitaea*	
Clossiana	*Mellicta*	

At first glance, specimens of the species included in these different genera look broadly similar, and it is only a detailed examination which reveals some of the different characters used to place the species in different genera.

For the purpose of this book the European butterflies are grouped into nine families, which is the more widely accepted grouping in popular field guide books. Some of the differences which separate the families are in characters which need to be examined under a lens. These are mentioned in the discussion about the families which follows, but the main features for recognition in the field are given first. Then, general notes on the caterpillars of that family are provided, followed by details on specific, noteworthy butterflies. In order to give general guidance fairly broad statements about the families are made. Inevitably there are exceptions to these statements and only a few of these can be discussed; others will be found in field guides. There is no better way of acquiring a basic understanding of the limits of each family than to look at collections of butterflies in your local museums. Most museums will have a collection and this will usually be arranged in a sequence of families. Illustrations in field guides will also give you an idea of the butterflies in each family and both sources should help you to recognise the appearance of the commoner species. The drawings accompanying the family outlines show representative species of each family. The sequence of families also varies in different books with some (as here) starting with the more primitive species, the Hesperiidae or skippers, and others with the Papilionidae or swallowtails. Only one of the following families, the Libytheidae, is not represented in Britain.

Skippers or awl butterflies Family Hesperiidae

This is a large family of generally small butterflies with wingspans varying from 18 to 36 mm in Europe. Skippers get their name from their characteristic swift, darting flight and when they rest they tend to sit more like moths than butterflies. They have relatively large bodies and heads and their antennae, which are widely separated at the base, end in a point. Skippers are usually found in grassy meadows and forest rides. The wing veins are unbranched beyond the cell (see figure 12). In some species there are large tufts of scales on the hind legs of the males. All have six functional legs in the adult but in the males the forelegs are slightly shorter than the hind. In many species the antennae are bent backwards slightly at the apex. The family has over thirty species in Europe but only eleven occur in Britain, of which eight are resident.

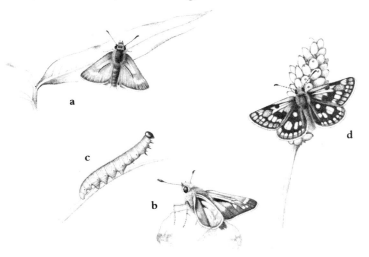

Figure 26 Representative species of family Hesperiidae. Male Lulworth Skipper (**a**); Male Silver-spotted Skipper (**b**) and caterpillar (**c**); Male Chequered Skipper (**d**)

Skippers often rest on the ground or on low vegetation, and will rise rapidly from this if disturbed or to chase another passing insect. These pursuit flights look quite aggressive but they seem to be all show. Most of the European skippers are rather dull by comparison with other butterflies but if examined closely some reveal quite intricate patterns. Many are not easy to identify in the field but a few of the commoner species are distinctive. When caught in a net they are difficult to handle and although more easily examined in a jar, they are so active that they may damage themselves.

Skipper caterpillars have large, rounded heads followed by a rather slender 'neck'. They usually taper at both ends and have smooth skins, although when looked at under a hand lens, short hairs can be seen. They live on grass and other herbaceous plants, generally rolling the leaves together to live inside a tube which they hold together with their silk. Some species live under a silken web. Their chrysalids differ from those of most other butterflies in being wrapped in a loosely spun cocoon.

For the butterfly watcher there are several distinctive common species like the Dingy Skipper which, despite its name, is quite well patterned, the Large Skipper (see figure 42), and the Large Chequered Skipper which is present in continental Europe only. The smaller number of species in Britain makes identification reasonably easy. The Essex Skipper and the Small Skipper, however, differ in the colour on the underside of the antennae, and in the extent of the sex brand on the wing in the male (see page 23): details which are not actually much help when trying to identify the flying insect. Most species of Hesperiidae in the world are relatively small and dull coloured. There are a few larger (up to 90 mm wingspan) and more brightly coloured species, but these are exceptions.

Swallowtails Family Papilionidae

Swallowtails are generally large butterflies with wingspans of 44 to 84 mm in the European species. They are mostly yellow and black with some, like the festoons and the apollos, having red on the wings. All species have three functional pairs of legs in the adult. Some of the veins on the

Figure 27 Swallowtail and caterpillar

forewings are branched beyond the cell and there is only one anal vein in the hindwing (see figure 12). Many of the species have tails to the hindwings (see figure 60), like the swallowtails, but the festoons and apollos which lack the tails, are very distinctively patterned species and unlikely to be confused with any others. Swallowtails do not have a fast flight and some species in particular have a relatively slow, flapping flight, compared with the swiftness and power of a Red Admiral or the larger fritillaries. They will often refuse to fly in what appear to be suitable weather conditions.

There are over 600 species of swallowtails found all over the world. They occur mainly in the tropics but a few are found in the more temperate regions. They include many colourful species, for example, the large, striking birdwing butterflies of South East Asia. There are eleven species in Europe but only one of these, the Swallowtail, is a resident in Britain. Four of the European species have been caught in Britain but their occurrence was accidental and they are not likely to be seen here.

The caterpillars of the swallowtails have an eversible, forked process on the back behind the head (see figure 16). This structure, the osmaterium, produces a strong scent and is believed to be a protective device against parasitic insects and predators. Many tropical swallowtail caterpillars feed on poisonous or distasteful plants, which make them distasteful (even poisonous perhaps) to predators, and they are also able to pass on the plant toxins to the adult butterfly. Since they are not good to eat, both the caterpillars and the butterflies can be colourful with lots of red and yellow, colours which warn predators they are distasteful. Caterpillars of the European species feed on umbelliferous plants like Wild Carrot and Fennel, as well as Birthwort, *Corydalis, Saxifrage*, Mountain House-leek and Stonecrop. The Swallowtail caterpillar in Britain feeds on Milk Parsley and other umbellifers. The caterpillar itself is bright green with black stripes and red spots.

Adult British Swallowtails are slightly different in colour and pattern from continental specimens. In British specimens the broad black band below the wing margin has a wavy outline, and is curved between each vein. In continental swallowtails this band is straight between each vein, and the whole black band on the wing therefore has roughly parallel sides. The yellow of these swallowtails is generally paler than those which live in East Anglia. The British Swallowtail is sufficiently distinct to have been given a subspecific name, *Papilio machaon britannicus. Machaon* is the specific name while *britannicus*, the subspecific name, signifies a small difference in the population which lives in Britain. In the tropics some of the colourful hindwings have a wingspan of 250 mm or more, while many of the others are much larger than swallowtails found in Europe. While there are a few closely allied and rather similar species in Europe, like the Southern Swallowtail and the Scarce Swallowtail, most species in this family are sufficiently large and colourful to be easily recognised on the wing.

Whites and yellows Family Pieridae

Some of the most common and best known butterflies are members of this worldwide family. These butterflies are medium sized with wing-spans ranging from 30 to 64 mm in Europe. As the family name implies they are generally white or yellow in colour and this coloration is due to pigments derived from a waste product of their metabolism. They include some of the few species of butterflies which are crop pests. Both

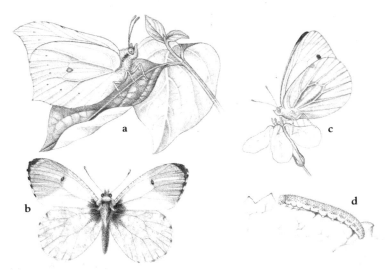

Figure 28 Representative species of family Pieridae. Brimstone (**a**); male Orange Tip (**b**); Green-veined White (**c**) and caterpillar (**d**)

sexes have three pairs of legs which are well developed and used for walking. The tip of each leg has four tiny forked claws best seen under a lens. There are two anal veins in the hindwings and the wings on their inner edges form a sort of groove into which the body fits. The only species likely to be confused with the whites and yellows (sometimes called sulphurs) is the Marbled White which, although predominantly black and white, is not a true white and has only two pairs of functional walking legs. It belongs in fact to the family Satyridae. The flight of whites and yellows is quite rapid interspersed with a more fluttering action, and they are especially attracted to white objects like pieces of paper, presumably mistaking them for white butterflies. In Europe there are over thirty-five species but only four of these are found in Britain, apart from some rare immigrants from the Continent.

Many of the pierids are migratory, travelling long distances to the northern parts of Europe to breed. They cannot survive the winter there and die out to be replaced in the following spring by new immigrants from further south. The caterpillars feed on plants of the families Cruciferae (including Cabbage), Leguminosae (includes clovers), Rhamnaceae (includes buckthorns) and Rosaceae (includes cherries). The Large or Cabbage White and Small White (the latter sometimes called the Small Cabbage White) can be serious pests of cabbages, their caterpillars stripping the plants to bare skeletons. The Small White has been introduced to a number of countries including North America and Australia. The Black-veined White, which formerly occurred in Britain, is now a rare migrant although on the continent its caterpillars can be pests of fruit trees.

The eggs of many species in the family are bottle-shaped (see figure 13) taller than they are wide. Pierid caterpillars are generally smooth and greenish, tapering towards the ends (see figure 19). Some species have gregarious larvae, others live singly. The chrysalis is generally angular, tapering to a point or points, at the head end. It is fastened by the tail hook (cremaster) and has a thin girdle of silk around the middle.

The Wood White and related species have probably one of the slowest and most fluttering flights of all the butterflies in Europe, and are found in woodland clearings. The white butterflies seen in spring and summer in gardens and parks, even in large towns, are generally Large or Cabbage Whites (see figure 12), Small Whites or the rather similar Green-veined Whites. The latter do not generally eat Cabbage and can be distinguished by the green colour and dark-lined veins on the underside of the hind wing (see figure 70). In continental Europe Green-veined Whites are very common and there are several other similar species.

In recent years another very attractive pierid, the Orange Tip, has become more common in Britain. It was more frequently seen in damper places but it has now spread to suburban parks and gardens. The male has the orange tip to the forewings (see figure 28), the female has a dusky tip to the wing.

Amongst the yellows there are a number of very similar species. The pattern and extent of black around the wings on the upperside and the underside hindwing separates these species, and so they have to be examined more closely, which is no easy task as they fly quickly by. In Britain and most of Europe any yellow butterfly in early spring will be a Brimstone. Later, the darker yellow-and-black Clouded Yellows cross the Channel and may be found flying around fields of clover. The commonest in Britain, the Clouded Yellow, occurs in varying numbers but is sometimes so abundant that these years are known as 'Clouded Yellow years' to lepidopterists. The Bath White is one of the rarer migrants to Britain, although it is fairly widespread in central and southern Europe, and like the Orange Tip, has a greenish underside to the hindwing (but lacks the orange on the forewing). Its popular name is said to come from an embroidery depicting this species worked by a 'Lady of Bath' in the eighteenth century.

Monarch or milkweeds Family Danaidae

Of this mainly tropical family the species that occasionally reaches Europe is unmistakeable. The Monarch has a wingspan of nearly 100 mm and is reddish brown with black veins, and a black-and-white wing margin. The second species, the Plain Tiger, which occurs in the Canary Islands and has been seen in Greece and Southern Italy, is smaller with a wingspan of up to 80 mm. It is also a tawny colour but the black veins are not so strongly marked, and it has a row of large white spots below the apex of the forewing. These butterflies have a rather lazy, flapping flight and as their bright coloration suggests they are distasteful to birds.

The Monarch is an occasional trans-Atlantic migrant to Europe from America. In Canada and the United States it is common and makes one of the most spectacular migrations of any butterfly, from Mexico to the far north in Alaska. It is also found in Australia and New Zealand. In recent years it has bred in the Canary Islands and these populations may be the source of some of the European individuals.

The Monarch caterpillar feeds on Milkweed and displays a warning coloration with yellow, black-and-white vertical stripes indicating it is distasteful. It has two long black filaments on the back of the thorax and two more near the tail. The pupae have several metallic spots and hang head downards from a small pad of silk spun by the caterpillar.

The forelegs of the adults are modified and not used for walking. The male butterfly has a pair of 'hair-pencils', tufts of extrusible scales, concealed in the tip of the abdomen. These are everted during courtship and produce a fairly pungent odour. The Monarch was formerly called, very descriptively, the Black-veined Brown. Its size attracts attention and the few individuals that reach Europe are soon caught by collectors. The story of its fascinating migration has been told in the book *The Monarch Butterfly* by F.A. Urquhart, and recently in the *Year of the Butterfly* by George Ordish. In parts of America the crowds of migrating Monarch butterflies resting on trees are a tourist attraction, and as such the butterflies are protected by law.

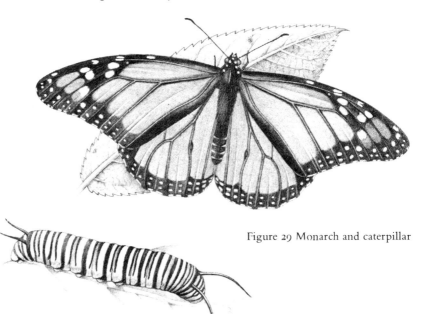

Figure 29 Monarch and caterpillar

Snout butterflies Family Libytheidae

A number of butterflies in this family are migrants and occur on every continent. They are readily recognisable by the long palps below the head which stick out like a snout. The single species in Europe, the Nettle Tree butterfly, is found only in southern France, Spain, Italy and south-eastern Europe. It is recognised both by its snout and by the very angular wings. The males have only two pairs of functional walking legs, the females have three pairs. The caterpillars feed on the Nettle Tree and the adult butterflies hibernate over the winter months.

Figure 30 Nettle Tree butterfly and caterpillar

Brush-footed butterflies Family Nymphalidae

This large and colourful family of butterflies found all over the world includes the fritillaries, admirals, emperors and vanessas. The adult butterflies in both sexes have only two pairs of walking legs, with the forelegs, not used for walking, often covered with tufts of scales, giving the name brush-footed. With the exception of the fritillaries, the outer margins of the wings are often angular or sharply indented. There are two anal veins in the hindwings. Most of the species have a very swift and powerful flight and many are among the commoner and better known of our butterflies; for example, the Small Tortoiseshell, Peacock and Red Admiral, and the rare but beautiful Purple Emperor.

Some of the most colourful butterflies, including many species sold in displays of butterflies for wall decorations, belong to this family. The South American *Morpho* butterflies include the huge metallic blue species with wingspans up to 160 mm. Their wings are often used in jewellery, and it is said that some six million specimens of one species are 'harvested' every year. In this species it is fortunately only the male that is the attractive metallic blue colour and the females are not collected. Other tropical nymphalids include the owl butterflies, dusk-flying butterflies with large eyespots on the underside of the wings. In Europe, the nymphalids have wingspans ranging from 28 to 82 mm. There are nearly seventy species in Europe of which over thirty species are recorded in Britain. A number of these are very rare migrants, however.

The caterpillars are generally covered in long bristly spines although different types, like the Purple Emperor, lack spines but possess two long horns over the head and a forked tail. They feed on a variety of plants including Nettle on which they are common, thistles, violets, Bilberry, Bramble, knapweed and Willow. The pupae are usually angular and often have silver or gold spots on them (see figure 25). The word chrysalis means 'golden' and is now applied generally to all butterflies.

Purple Emperors are not often seen because they tend to keep near

Figure 31 Representative species of family Nymphalidae. Small Tortoiseshell (**a**) and caterpillar (**b**); Marsh Fritillary (**c**); White Admiral (**d**)

the higher branches of trees. They return to their favourite spot high up on an Oak tree over and over again. Their feeding habits are unlike most other butterflies because instead of nectar they feed on decaying animals, or the liquid ooze from pigsties. The females fly lower down in the woods and will swoop down, harmlessly, on passers-by.

Many nymphalid butterflies have a dark coloured underside, well camouflaged against the ground when they land. The Comma, with its ragged wings and leaf-like underside is one of the most successful in this respect, its irregular outline helping it to disappear into its background (see figure 72). The Two-tailed Pasha is a species found in the southern part of Europe. It is the only representative of a widespread African group and is a large butterfly (wingspan 78 to 82 mm) with two tails on each hindwing. The admiral butterflies (*Vanessa* species) are mostly black with white bands and patches. They and the related gliders (*Neptis* species) have a very distinctive flight with alternate flapping and gliding. The Camberwell Beauty is rare in Britain and is a more northern species. It is a striking butterfly with a dark purplish wing and a broad creamy border. The conspicuous Painted Lady is a migrant, a fast-flying species which, like the Red Admiral, cannot survive the northern winter. In spring it moves north from Africa and southern Europe to Britain and Scandinavia.

Most of the nymphalids mentioned so far are relatively easy for the butterfly watcher to identify on the wing. Now we come to the fritillaries, a more difficult but equally interesting group. In the main they are orange-brown with darker marks on the upperside. The undersides are similarly patterned but paler, and the underside hindwing has diagnostic patterns. The Cardinal is a large fritillary with a wingspan of 64 to 80 mm, and while broadly similar to the others, it has a characteristic reddish patch on the underside of the forewing. It occurs rarely in Britain and could be mistaken for a Silver-washed Fritillary, although the latter lacks the rosy red underwing.

In Britain, where there are less than a dozen common fritillary species, a good look at the underside of the butterfly as it sits on a flower will enable you to identify it. If you are quick, for most are fast fliers, fritillaries can be caught and examined more closely in the net. Fritillaries are common but will not be easily seen until their favourite haunts are discovered. Some, like the Marsh Fritillary, occur in small, usually isolated, colonies. A number of species, like Frigga's and Frejya's Fritillaries, are not found in Britain, and live in moorland bogs. The Glanville Fritillary in Britain is known only from the Isle of Wight and has a celebrated name. This species was named after a Mrs Glanville, an eighteenth century butterfly collector, whose will was contested on the grounds of insanity, the alleged proof of which lay in the fact that she collected butterflies!

Browns and satyrs Family Satyridae

At first sight these are the most dull of the butterfly families but close inspection will reveal subtle and intricate patterns on their wings. They usually have white and black-ringed eyespots and these can sometimes be very large and conspicuous. Most have a rather gentle flight, certainly not showing the power of the nymphalids. Many are shade-loving woodland and meadow butterflies and a few tropical species fly at dusk. The underside pattern of the wings is excellent camouflage when they are at rest with wings closed above the body. One of the exceptions to this is the Marbled White. This butterfly may be distinguished from the whites of the family Pieridae by the fact that it has only two pairs of functional legs, and rather more black scales on the wings. The Satyridae, like the Nymphalidae, have only two pairs of walking legs and two anal veins in the hind wings. Apart from colour and pattern, however, their most distinctive character is the swollen base to the veins in the forewing

Figure 32 Representative species of family Satyridae. Marbled White (**a**) and caterpillar
(**b**); Small Heath (**c**); Meadow Brown (**d**)

with one, two or even three veins dilated where they arise at the base of
the wing (see figure 32d). Once you have studied illustrations and
museum specimens to familiarise yourself with the overall characteristics,
it is not difficult to recognise a member of the Satyridae in the field, but it
is very difficult if not impossible to separate individual species. However,
some which are so hard to identify on pattern, even as pinned specimens
in a collection, often have very distinctive behaviour or habitat preferences. The Satyridae are a worldwide group with some species found as
far north as the subarctic. In continental Europe over 100 species display
rather similar patterns; in Britain we have eleven species some of which
are very common, and four others whose occurrence is accidental. The
European Satyridae range in wingspan from 27 to 78 mm.

Satyrid caterpillars taper at both ends and often have two small points
at one end rather like a forked tail. Most feed on grasses, some fairly
generally and others with more restricted feeding. The chrysalids are
mostly blunt-ended and do not have any spines or angular projections
(see figure 25).

Some of the common satyrid butterflies, like the Meadow Brown,
Speckled Wood and Grayling, are widespread and the Meadow Brown is
often abundant on grasslands, flying even in overcast weather. Although
there is only one species of Marbled White in Britain there are several on
the continent, and this is true for most of the British butterflies. In Britain,
the Grayling is a species that prefers open ground but its relative the Tree

Grayling is a woodland species, often found in open pinewoods on heathlands. The Rock Grayling, which does not occur in Britain, lives in central and southern Europe in drier mountain areas. There is an enormous group of satyrids called ringlets, many of which live in the mountains, which are characterised by eyespots on the wings and difficult to identify by pattern alone. A related group, the heaths, are broadly similar to one another in pattern, and the undersides of their wings have to be examined closely to be certain of correct identification. Fortunately for most butterfly watchers the common species will provide sufficient source of interest and practice in identification, and the more difficult species can be left until more experience has been gained.

Metalmarks Family Nemeobiidae (Riodinidae)

Metalmarks are particularly common in South America where they are some of the most colourful butterflies with bright metallic hues. Only one species of this tropical family occurs in Europe. This is the Duke of Burgundy's Fritillary, which is not a fritillary at all, but named as such because its pattern is slightly reminiscent of that group. The male has its forelegs reduced and not used for walking but all three pairs are functional in the female. The Duke of Burgundy's Fritillary is found in woodlands where its flight is described as a 'giddy zig-zag, settling more on leaves than on flowers'. Its 28 to 34 mm wingspan will distinguish it from the Marsh Fritillary (34 to 38 mm), whose pattern is similar. In flight, however, it can resemble a dark specimen of the Small Copper. The caterpillar is shaped rather like a woodlouse, tapering at both ends (see figure 33). It feeds on Primrose and Cowslip.

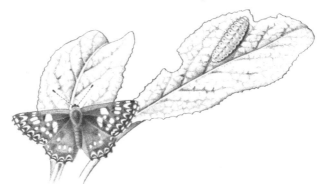

Figure 33 Duke of Burgundy Fritillary and caterpillar.

Blues, hairstreaks and coppers Family Lycaenidae

These are generally rather small butterflies often with metallic colours on the upperside and delicate patterns on the underside. Many are rather similar and need careful examination to distinguish them from closely allied species. The sexes differ in the blues with the females usually brown, sometimes with a few blue scales. The hairstreaks usually have thin white lines, from which they get their names, on the underside of the wings, where the blues have delicate rows of spots. The coppers, as their name implies, are usually a bronze or copper colour on the upperside of the wings. Lycaenids have three pairs of functional legs although the fore-legs of the males are shorter than the other two pairs. They usually have one or two less veins in the forewing than members of other families. They are relatively small but many of them can fly quite fast over the ground. They often settle in dull weather with their heads downward on

Figure 34 Representative species of family Lycaenidae. Small Copper (**a**); Brown Hairstreak (**b**); Holly blue (**c**) and caterpillar (**d**)

grass stems or other low-growing plants (see figure 56). Others have low, jerky flights as they go from flower to flower, and are found together in numbers. The family is world wide, being particularly common in the rain forests of South East Asia and Africa. There are some ninety species in Europe of which nineteen are found in Britain, but several of these are rare and one is now extinct. Lycaenid butterflies in Europe range in size from 18 to 42 mm wingspan. While the upperside gives you a guide to the main grouping, it is often the details on the underside hindwing which are diagnostic for the species.

Lycaenid caterpillars are shaped rather like woodlice with small heads that can be retracted. Many have special glands which produce a sweet secretion attractive to ants and in some, the Large Blue for example, this relationship is taken to the extreme with the caterpillar living in the ants' nest and feeding on ant larvae. Some caterpillars live inside the pods of legumes, an unusual place for the larvae of a butterfly which tends to live in more open situations. The caterpillars of lycaenid butterflies feed on flowers, fruit, docks and leguminous plants. The chrysalids are small and rounded, without spines or angles and some produce a sound, although the significance of this is not understood.

The hairstreaks include the Green Hairstreak which, like its relative the Chapman's Green Hairstreak, has a green underside to the fore- and hindwings (see figure 23). The latter species occurs in a few places in the South of France and Iberia. The coppers have only one common species in Britain, the Small Copper, but there are many species on the Continent. The British Large Copper, whose caterpillars fed on Great Water Dock, lived in the fenlands but became extinct in the mid-nineteenth century. In spite of their small size some of the blues are migratory, including the Long-tailed and Short-tailed Blue, both are migrants to Britain. Many of the blues have short tails on the hindwings with small spots close by. When the butterfly is at rest with the wings over the body, the combination of the spots looking like eyes and tails quivering like antennae, gives the impression of a head. It is possible that this would distract predators from the real head; a bird pecking at this tail would almost certainly get only a fragment of wing, and the butterfly would most likely escape. Some of the blues live in isolated colonies and the individuals can often develop small pattern or colour differences from individuals in other colonies. Providing the differences are maintained over the years subspecific names are often given to these slightly different populations.

Field guides and identification

Most field guides portray butterflies in formal 'pinned' attitudes; few show the insects in the position in which they will be seen in the field. The identification of a butterfly flitting between flowers from the illustration in a field guide is therefore quite a challenge. A further problem encountered with identification occurs when descriptions of a butterfly from two people who have seen the same insect rarely agree. When I describe a flower to a botanist, a look of despair usually appears on his face as he tries to make sense of my description!

Field guides and museum specimens help you to learn the characteristic colour, pattern and shape of a species, and to know what to look for in the field. It is not so useful, however, when looking at field guides merely to notice that there are differences between two closely related butterflies. It is unlikely, when you see them, that they will be flying side by side for comparison! It is therefore necessary to study the particular characters of the pattern of the species (two silver spots instead of three perhaps) which distinguish it from related species. A few butterflies are so distinctively marked that once you have seen them in flight, or settled on a plant, you will be able to find them easily in a field guide. With the majority, however, remember that they will not normally be sitting with their wings spread out as shown in the illustrations.

Each field guide has its advantages and disadvantages. Some cover only the more common species. This is a good start but a beginner's book will probably not cover the variation you may reasonably expect to see. Other guides which are reasonably comprehensive for Europe are too

Figure 35 At first glance the upperside of the Pearl-bordered Fritillary (**a**) and Small Pearl-bordered Fritillary (**b**) look very similar. With practice they can be separated in the field by the slight difference in the underside pattern.

daunting for most people, and tend to conceal the common species in a plethora of rarities. Field guides with paintings showing the pattern of upperside and underside are excellent, but can be a little confusing to use at first. The underside of the forewing is rarely seen until the butterfly is pinned for a collection. Pinned butterflies are set to display the wings and always have them pinned forward. In a correctly set butterfly the hind margin of the forewing should be at right-angles to the body, which explains the slightly unnatural position.

Field guides with photographs of the living insect are probably most help at first, providing you can see, or the text points out, the characters used for identifying the species. In other words, photographs are fine as long as the distinction of that species from a closely allied one is clearly indicated, for example, by an arrow, or it is mentioned in the text. Most butterfly field guides are arranged by families, and this is useful because it shows related and similar species together. Others deal with habitats and the associated species to be found in them. They are all helpful in their ways although one single guide cannot answer all the queries. The size of the European fauna with some 400 species makes it impractical to expect all the varieties and subspecies to be covered in one book. In the British fauna with less than 100 species, of which only fifty to sixty breed, a wider range of figures of the various forms is possible. Whole books have been devoted to aberrations of one species of British butterfly.

The dimensions of butterflies given in field guides may differ by only a few millimetres between species and therefore appear insignificant. It is surprising how obvious these differences become when you start watching the various species in the field. Guide books vary in the way they show the measurements of wings. Many books give, for example, 'wing

10 mm'. This is the measurement from the apex or tip of the forewing to the base of the same wing where it joins the body. The wingspan, from wingtip to wingtip, is therefore approximately twice this figure. Other books give the wingspan, the distance between the apex, or the outer margins of the wings if these bulge outwards. Wingspan is measured on set museum specimens and as butterflies do not naturally spread their wings in the same way in the field, this measurement can only be used as an approximate guide.

Many books provide a checklist of species, often including some that are not illustrated. This is not as pointless as it might appear at first for consider this possibility. A butterfly may be seen which resembles one of the illustrations, a Clouded Yellow for example, but which does not match exactly. Look at the scientific name and especially the first, generic, name. For the Clouded Yellow it would be *Colias croceus*. Under the checklist look up the genus *Colias*, where you will see not only *croceus* but several other *Colias* species listed. If it is a comprehensive list of European species there will be twelve names in the genus. Then, look up the distribution (this is given in *A field guide to the Butterflies of Britain and Europe* (1970) and the *Hamlyn nature guide Butterflies* (1979)) where you will see that a number of *Colias* species are known only from Scandinavia or southern Europe. While it may not be possible to identify your speci-men exactly in the absence of a figure, you can probably get near to it, and can look it up in one of the more comprehensive works (see Further reading). Wherever you are, the basic tenet is always to expect the unexpected, but to remember that the butterfly you see is more likely to be the common, widely distributed one.

Foodplants given in the guides can help in deciding on the species. A female butterfly (unless on migration) is quite likely to be somewhere near the foodplant of its caterpillar, and the males will not be far away. Distribution maps, while useful, can be misleading. Many species have favourite habitats and these are often not evenly distributed. The map may well show a solid area throughout Europe, however, and so the distribution must then be interpreted as European in suitable localities. Other maps may show the species distribution dotted about which suggests that the butterflies are not found in all suitable localities and are restricted in some other way.

You will find that the terms used in most books will be explained; the symbols ♂ for males and ♀ for females are used internationally in zoology. Sometimes the expression type locality is used. This is the area from which the species was originally described. Some of the species described by Linnaeus which he collected himself may have a type locality in Sweden, where he lived. Other terms like ground colour (of the wing) will be defined according to the author's usage. This is generally the background colour on to which one imagines the other colours and pattern have been added.

4 Where to find butterflies

As your interest in butterflies increases you will find that you are concerned not only with the identification of species, but also with the relationship of those species to the places in which they are found. You are now becoming interested in the 'ecology' of butterflies and the sort of questions that now arise are: Why is this particular species in this particular place? What keeps it here? Why is it not more (or less) abundant? What causes its numbers to fluctuate over the year? Why is it always seen with certain other species?

Some of the answers are of course self-evident. For example, in its first generation each year, the Holly Blue is associated with Holly and you would expect to find it somewhere near the plant. The next generation, however, lives on Ivy so be a little wary of popular names and their implications when looking for answers. Sometimes an apparently suitable habitat with the right food for the caterpillars and nectar for the adults

Figure 36 Most of the broad-leaved plants at the foot of this hedgerow have been killed by a herbicide spray. Among these plants will be many caterpillar foodplants.

Figure 37 The beautiful Apollo butterfly is now protected by law in many parts of Europe and a licence from the country of origin is needed to trade internationally in specimens. It is widespread but not common in some hilly areas of Europe and is very rare in Britain.

will not have the butterflies one might expect. The answers here might be related to the recent history of the habitat. A heath fire one or more years ago, for example, may have caused local extinction of a species and the butterfly may not yet have spread back into the now recovered habitat. If you can follow the recovery of a habitat after a fire or flood, or some other cause, you can gain a useful insight into the rate of recovery and spread of the species. After a fire some butterflies, like Graylings and Small Heaths, move back in almost before the ground is cool. If a very large area has been burnt recovery may be quite slow as the re-invasion takes place from all round the perimeter.

Man-made problems can affect large areas. The drift of an insecticidal spray from a nearby field, or as the result of an aerial spraying programme, can be extensive and can destroy all the insects in a locality. If the insecticide is persistent its effect may last several months, but this will only be apparent by the lack of insects or a reduction in their numbers, for the vegetation itself may well thrive. Herbicides which are sprayed can have a similar long-term effect, but they kill off many of the plants on which caterpillars would feed, and so these just starve (see figure 36).

Another 'historic' event which may have affected a habitat is a particularly severe winter. This usually results in less insect life due either to the direct effect of the cold on the overwintering stages, or to the increased efforts of warm-blooded mammals and birds to find food in prolonged cold weather, and eating more overwintering insects. Sometimes the converse of this is reported, when the severe winter with snow-covered ground prevents predatory animals from getting at the insects, and so more of the latter survive. It is as well to remember, however, that the reason for abundance or scarcity of a species is rarely due to any single factor acting on its own.

As you study butterflies you will get more experienced in recognising the signs which tell you they are present in a particular locality, and this will help you to predict where else you may find them. Most of this information comes from plant associations. You will find it a tremendous advantage if you can recognise by sight, if not by name, combinations of plants which are important to the species. The actual presence of a particular species when the adult is not flying is more difficult to detect.

Figure 38 The Clouded Yellow is seen only as a summer visitor from southern Europe for it cannot survive the winter in northern Europe. In some years this butterfly is common in Britain and northern Europe and large numbers may be seen over fields of Clover or Lucerne.

Figure 39 (Photograph on page 62) The widespread Meadow Brown butterfly, feeding on Stonecrop. This butterfly is one of the more common species in meadows, downlands and grassy areas, but also occurs in other habitats.

Figure 42 Spiders are an ever-present danger to butterflies. Crab spiders sit and wait for their prey on flower heads, and this one has just pounced on a Large Skipper.

You must look for signs of the activity of the caterpillars with webbing, chewed or rolled leaves and frass, being the most obvious features.

In Britain it has been found that the distribution of many species is correlated with summer temperature, and that change in distribution over the years is due to fluctuations in the mean temperature. When you think about it, butterflies (and other animals) are not evenly spread over the countryside but occur in groups. Why is this? To understand something of the distribution of butterflies it is as well to be aware of the distribution of the plants with which they are associated. The Chalk-hill Blue and Adonis Blue, for example, are restricted to areas with limestone or chalk, although they do not occur in all the areas with these formations. In this case it is the presence or absence of the main chalk-loving food-plant, Horseshoe Vetch, which probably accounts for their distribution. Butterflies owe their first allegiance to plants, and in fact the whole of the plant-butterfly relationship is a result of the complex interaction of their joint evolution over millions of years.

Sometimes the plants on which the caterpillar feeds are close together. Then, if one plant is stripped by a brood of caterpillars, there is a good chance that they will find another nearby after crawling only a short distance. Imagine the hazards facing a caterpillar, however, as it leaves the plant on which it has been feeding to look for a fresh plant. The original hostplant on which the egg was laid may have died, dried up, been damaged by some other insect, or just overwhelmed by a massive attack of caterpillars. Much of the search for the new foodplant seems to be a random wandering, and little research has been done on the orientation of caterpillars in these circumstances. When the hostplant dies the hungry caterpillar will have a limited time to find food, avoiding predators on the way, and its sense of smell probably plays a part. Caterpillars crawling through the 'jungle' surrounding their foodplant seem to have a limited range for searching, and many do not seem to be able to find a new foodplant further than three metres away. The density as well as the abundance of the foodplants may also therefore be an important factor in the survival of the caterpillars, and consequently the size of the butterfly population.

What makes a species rare? We talk freely about rare species but with few exceptions these are common elsewhere. The whole idea of finding rare animals (or plants) has been and still is one of the main driving forces

Figure 40 (Photographs on page 63) The Chalk-hill Blue is a very variable species and a whole book has been devoted to descriptions of its many variations of pattern and colour. Here a male is shown in its chalk grassland habitat.

Figure 41 The male Adonis Blue is a deep blue colour but the female here has much more brown on the wing. This butterfly is restricted to limestone areas where the foodplant of the caterpillar is Horseshoe Vetch. Note the misshapen hindwing in this specimen, probably due to the wing not expanding fully on emergence from the chrysalis.

behind those who prefer to collect specimens. Even now we spend a lot of time and money and arouse a lot of public interest on the subject of rarities. In the case of the Ospreys nesting in Scotland, the publicity surrounding these rare birds has been put to good use. Here the interest stimulated brings in funds to support the birds' protection and the publicised nest takes the pressure off other breeding pairs, which can nest in peace. Unfortunately, most butterflies do not breed at the top of trees, and so in the case of a very rare species, the less disturbance and publicity the butterflies receive the better. Rarity in one area may be the result of many different factors including scarcity of suitable habitats or host-plants, an excess of parasites or predators, or climatic fluctuations which are unsuitable for the species. There are usually several contributing factors rather than one single cause, but sometimes the reason may be simply that the butterfly is secretive in its habits and we have just over-looked it.

For the ecologist the questions to be asked about the rarity of a species are many. Suitability of habitat is easy to assess and is answered by the question: Are the plants with which the butterfly is usually associated present in the habitat being studied? If the habitat is suitable: Is this a year in which predation has been particularly high? The question of whether a cold winter favours or acts against the insects has already been mentioned. Parasites of butterflies can have a surprisingly dramatic effect on population size, and it is interesting that it can be the climate that plays a vital but indirect part in affecting the numbers of host and parasite. Research on the Mymarid parasite of Leafhopper eggs, for example, has shown that the development of its larvae is accelerated by a cool spring, resulting in the same generation of Leafhopper eggs being parasitized twice. In such years Leafhopper numbers are very low and Mymarid parasites high. However, rarity caused indirectly by special factors cannot be identified without a detailed study of the life-history and biology of the butterfly and its parasites, and is therefore a more appropriate subject for study by the scientist rather than the butterfly watcher.

Rarity which is a feature of a butterfly on the edge of its range has already been mentioned. A population of insects fluctuates with pressures to expand if more adults survive, or contract if fewer adult survive. A stable population probably does not exist in nature. In some butterfly populations the mated females tend to move to the periphery of the main population, possibly to avoid more encounters with males. This is also a good mechanism to help extend the range of the species, and to colonise new habitats on the edge of the range if conditions are suitable.

In Britain the rarity of many species is due to them being on the edge of their European range. Such small populations are vulnerable and small climatic changes may reduce a population to a point where males and females do not meet, or only a few matings take place. Without new immigrants from the Continent, where the butterflies may also be with-drawing, the impoverished populations will not last long. The Glanville

Fritillary has a very restricted distribution in Britain where it was formerly more widespread, and as the population falls on the Continent, so it does in Britain (though perhaps not always for the same reasons).

Butterflies, like people, are divided up into populations in particular areas, and populations of butterflies, like people, develop their own local characteristics. Butterfly populations are basically centred around their foodplants and barriers may exist between one population and a neighbouring one, to prevent them mixing. A barrier may be a river or merely a hedge, or a totally unsuitable area like a large urban development. It is always interesting to see if the butterflies you are watching have a definite territory within which they stay. Many do, and their dispersal within this area is over short distances, perhaps within one or two fields. There is a possibility but as far as I am aware no proof, that butterflies can learn the characteristic of their home area and recognise it. This has been suggested from the movements of individuals captured in one spot, released in another, and finding their way back to the first site. Certainly if a butterfly is hatched in the garden and kept there in a cage for a few days before release, it will often return to feed. Local differences in populations of butterflies can be important in preventing mixing with neighbouring ones. In fact, over a period of time, a biological difference may arise in one species spread over several areas which will prevent interbreeding from different populations even if they are artificially mixed. New subspecies or species may arise by this process.

In the following section a few of the butterflies associated with the major habitats are discussed. Many butterflies range over a wide variety of habitats: a few are very specific in their requirements. Details of the types of areas in which species will be found are given in most field guides (see Further reading). The foodplants of the caterpillars of some of the species mentioned in this section are to be found in Appendix I. Foodplants of the caterpillars of species not dealt with there are given here.

The woodland habitat

The two main woodland divisions considered here are broad-leaved deciduous woods and coniferous evergreen woods. There are many possible combinations of these and the composition of the woodland will have an effect on its suitability as a habitat for butterflies. Dense woodland with few open spaces, whether deciduous or coniferous, is not a good place for butterflies. The closeness of the trees in such woods restricts the available sunlight, so that there is often no undergrowth of flowers. Butterflies will also avoid the sheer physical density of the vegetation. Even the true woodland species prefer open glades and rides and the edges of clearings or streams rather than the denser parts.

In broad-leaved wooded areas, parkland with trees or small wooded copses are the places to look for woodland butterflies, apart from the rides in the main parts of the woods. The abundance of flowers and herbaceous undergrowth here is particularly attractive to butterflies. One

Figure 43 A wood with both coniferous (left) and broad-leaved (right) trees. The open areas with plenty of flowers along the paths will be especially favoured by butterflies but the dense coniferous trees with no undershrubs will not attract them.

woodland species, the Purple Emperor, lives in mixed woods with Oak and Beech but tends to keep high up in the trees. The Large Tortoiseshell is another butterfly associated with woodland edges and this species is particularly attracted (although not restricted) to Elm on which the caterpillar feeds. It is too early to predict how the loss of so many Elms through Dutch Elm disease will finally affect the Large Tortoiseshell populations in Britain, but they are certain to reduce even further. The arrival and rapid spread of this disease, a fungus which is distributed by a scolytid beetle, shows how easily species of plants, even large trees, can be devastated. The Large Tortoiseshell caterpillar will feed on other trees and so it may well survive this crisis, but it is not difficult to imagine what would happen to a species restricted to a plant destroyed in a similar epidemic.

The Lesser Purple Emperor is common in woodlands in continental Europe but absent from Britain, its caterpillar feeding on Willow and Poplar. The Purple Hairstreak is fairly common in Oakwoods as far north as southern Scandinavia but it is restricted and very local in England and Wales, and is found in only one or two localities in Scotland. White Admirals can be found in many woodlands in southern Britain and continental Europe. This is one of the species fond of flying in the more open parts of woods, especially where there are Brambles. Some of the fritillaries are woodland species, particularly where there are violets growing in the clearings. These include the Silver-washed, High Brown and, in spite of its name, Heath Fritillary. The latter occurs in woodlands in drier areas with poor soil, and will also be found in the sparse woods on heaths. The delicate Wood White lives in woodlands and woodland margins but occurs in larger forests on the Continent. Clearings in woodlands will attract the smaller fritillaries, the Pearl-bordered and the Small-pearl Bordered, although the latter prefers damper parts of the woods. The Speckled Wood occurs throughout woodlands over most of central and southern Britain and western Scotland, but is less common in the rest of the country. Although a woodland butterfly it is particularly attracted to patches of sunlight, especially if these have Brambles growing in them. The margins of woodlands, where the trees thin out and flowers grow in profusion, are always attractive to butterflies, and this is where the Duke of Burgundy Fritillary lives. This is a rather local species in Britain although it is quite widespread on the Continent.

As we have already mentioned, few butterflies will be found in dense coniferous plantations, unless there are open rides and clearings. Some of the more open pinewoods on heathland, however, are attractive to a number of species; the Scotch Argus, Small Heath and some of the smaller fritillaries prefer such habitats. The Large Wall Brown, Woodland Ringlet and Tree Grayling will be found in this type of area on the Continent. The caterpillars of these species feed on various grasses. The Grayling and Common Blue may well be seen on pine-clad heaths together with the Dark Green Fritillary.

The meadow and hedgerow habitat

The hedgerows which are so much a part of the British countryside are fast disappearing in many areas. Modern agricultural techniques demand larger fields for the economical production of food, and these requirements override the very real ecological value of hedges. When hedges remain spraying and mechanical cutting all weaken the varied plant life to be found in them. If you watch the plant growth in hedgerows (or any other habitat) you will know when to expect the butterflies to appear. In fact, there are few better places for butterflies than a hedgerow with a wide variety of flowers.

In early spring overwintering Small Tortoiseshells, Commas and Peacock butterflies, as well as the Brimstones, are tempted out to Hazel catkins. A little later in the spring or early summer, Orange Tips and Gatekeepers (more appropriately called Hedge Browns) will be seen flying up and down the lanes between the hedgerows. The Wall Brown will be sunning itself in more open patches, sitting with its wings spread wide out, and the ubiquitous Meadow Brown will certainly be there in season. The Green-veined White is a typical species of hedgerows and meadows and will be seen commonly in both. Both the smaller fritillaries, the Pearl-bordered and Small Pearl-bordered, are common in meadow-

Figure 44 The hedgerow in spring and summer with a profusion of flowers is a favourite butterfly habitat. It will attract Orange Tips, blues, browns and tortoiseshells.

lands. To see butterflies at their best in large numbers, however, the Alpine meadows of Europe with their abundant flowers should be visited. The blues, browns and the excitement of the occasional beautiful Apollo provide a memorable spectacle. There are many other places in central and southern Europe where the abundance of flowers is peculiarly attractive to butterflies. The 'Valley of the Butterflies' on the Island of Rhodes is a famous tourist attraction where many species are abundant in the spring and early summer. There may not be as many different species to be seen in the meadows of Britain and northern Europe, but these places are still splendid sites to watch butterflies in the summer months. Skipper butterflies are usually plentiful in season, whirring about in their characteristic flight, and the Brown Argus and Common Blue will also be seen.

The downland habitat

The chalk downlands of southern England and the Continent have certain species which are exclusive to these habitats; the Adonis Blue, Chalk-hill Blue and Silver-spotted Skipper, for example, are virtually restricted to these areas. The Silver-studded Blue may also be common on chalk downland but this butterfly has a wider distribution in Britain on more northerly limestone outcrops. There are also more widespread species here like the Meadow Brown, Red Admiral, Peacock and the Large and Small Skippers. There are a number of additional species to be found in limestone areas on the Continent, especially in southern Europe, and these include the Damon and Turquoise Blues, whose

Figure 45 The Adonis Blue, Chalk-hill Blue and Silver-spotted Skipper are restricted to the chalk downland habitat, which also attracts many of the more widespread species.

caterpillars feed on Sainfoin, Thyme, trefoils and related plants of the pea family.

In Britain the Marbled White tends to occur on chalky soils but it is more widespread on the Continent. Other species like the Common Blue, Brown Argus and the more local Small Blue, are also found on chalk downlands. The Grayling, although more widespread, is often common in limestone areas and this and the Silver-studded Blue form local and distinct subspecies in parts of Britain.

The mountain and moorland habitat

The Mountain Ringlet and Large Heath are true mountain butterflies in Britain and both occur in boggy areas in Scotland and the Lake District, although the Large Heath is also found further south in Wales. The Scotch Argus is another typical species associated with moorlands in northern Britain, especially near coniferous forests on hillsides. Moorlands are also a good place to find the Silver-studded Blue, while above cliffs the Dark Green Fritillary can usually be seen. There are many more mountain butterflies on the Continent. The ringlets are particularly associated with mountains and many, like the Lapland and the Arctic Ringlet, live in the far north of Europe. Their caterpillars are not well known but probably feed on species of grass. Further south on the drier hillsides the Southern Swallowtail, whose caterpillar feeds on Fennel, and the Sooty Satyr, whose caterpillar feeds on grasses, will be found. Butter-flies like Cynthia's Fritillary (Plantain and Alpine Lady's Mantle) and the Alpine Grayling (grasses) are more restricted in distribution and found in the Alps. The Green Hairstreak, which often occurs in lowland woods in southern Britain, may sometimes be found at over 2,000 metres on moorlands on the Continent.

Figure 46 A number of butterflies are found in moorland habitats including the Small Heath, Silver-studded Blue and Scotch Argus.

The marsh, lake and river habitat

In all the habitats discussed the foodplants are the first necessity for the butterflies. There must also be a total habitat effect, about which we know very little, to explain why one area has a particular species and another very similar one does not. In the marsh, lake and river habitat the cater-pillars of the Large Copper, for example, feed mainly on Great Water Dock, a plant described in the standard British flora as 'fairly generally

Figure 48 A Meadow Brown at rest among Beech leaves is equally well camouflaged and hidden from predators.

Figure 49 Birds are major predators of butterflies. A bird has evidently caught this Black Hairstreak in its beak but the butterfly was able to escape with wing damage.

distributed throughout the British Isles'. The British Large Copper, which was previously known only from the East Anglian fens, is now extinct and the introduced Dutch Large Copper, a related subspecies, survives in the fens in a restricted area. So it cannot be merely the availability of the foodplant which is the key to the distribution of this species. Some species like the Marsh Fritillary are partial to the wetter areas on moorlands but also occur on dry flowery slopes, providing the foodplants of the caterpillars are present. The Orange Tip and Green-veined White, together with other species, may also be found in marshy areas in Britain, but on the Continent this habitat holds a greater variety

Figure 51 The marshy fenland habitat supports the Large Copper and Swallowtail. Many other species are associated with this type of habitat on the Continent.

of species. Species occurring in the boggy ground of northern Europe are the Lapland, Cranberry and Bog Fritillaries, whose caterpillars feed on Cranberry and Whortleberry, and the Moorland Clouded Yellow which is commoner in damper parts of the Continent. Curiously enough, the Swallowtail, which in Britain is restricted to the East Anglian fens apart from the odd continental migrant which turns up further south, is

Figure 50 Red mites are often parasites on butterflies, attaching themselves to the body and piercing the skin to suck body fluid. On this Marbled White butterfly they are attached to the base of the thorax and abdomen, and at the thinner membrane behind the head.

more associated with meadows on the Continent. The Purple-edged Copper is one of the beautiful blues found in marsh areas in Europe, and is a species recorded in Britain in the seventeenth century. There seems to be some doubt about the authenticity of this report, however.

The seashore and coastal dunes habitat

The shoreline is not a place to normally search for butterflies although many migrants may be seen there, and Graylings will often stray from the nearby cliffs or dunes over the shore. In Britain three species, the Glanville Fritillary, Essex Skipper and Lulworth Skipper are primarily coastal. They also occur a little way inland but they are very local. On the Continent the same species are more widespread which makes the restriction to the coastal habitat in Britain puzzling. From nearby rough ground, or sand-dunes where the dunes have been fixed by Marram grass and other short grasses have taken over, the Common Blue, Meadow Brown, Small Heath and Small Copper will usually be found. Sea cliffs covered with vegetation often attract Dark Green Fritillaries and even Ringlets may live here in some areas.

Figure 52 On the seashore, where the dunes are fixed and the vegetation established, the Grayling, Common Blue and Meadow Brown will be found.

The town and gardens habitat

With the help of the keen gardener who grows the right kind of flowers (see page 118), gardens and flower-filled parks can be rich in butterflies. The whites are all too common, especially if you are trying to grow Cabbage, but do try to distinguish harmful species from good. The caterpillars of Large and Small Whites will eat Cabbage, but those of the Green-veined White will not. Small Tortoiseshells, Peacocks and Red

Figure 53 An Orange Tip rests with wings tightly closed to show its mottled green underside.

Admirals are always welcome in the garden, and they are frequent visitors even in the centre of towns. In recent years in Britain the Holly Blue has increased its distribution, and this delightful butterfly can be seen within a couple of miles of central London. The Orange Tip, which has always previously been regarded as a butterfly of damp meadows in the country, has also started to move into suburban gardens. In spring the unmistakeable Brimstone is widespread in gardens in central and southern Britain and throughout the Continent as far north as central Scandinavia.

5 How to watch butterflies

It is all very well sitting down to watch butterflies in a particular habitat but what are we looking for and how can we make use of our observations? Before we can begin to answer these questions, however, the first habit we must get into is that of recording exactly what we have seen. This is an important aspect of watching any form of wildlife and for butterflies it can vary from simply making entries in a diary of, for example, items like the first sighting of a butterfly in spring, to writing detailed notes about the behaviour of a particular species.

Recording what is seen

Writing notes or sketching has now been supplemented by the use of tape-recorders and cameras which give a wider choice of the methods available to record our data. Tape-recorders provide a marvellous opportunity to record information in the field and particularly of an event while it is happening. Unlike many animals, butterflies are rarely disturbed by the sound of voices and will ignore an observer talking into a microphone. Using a tape-recorder will also enable you to dictate notes about events which can happen suddenly, without taking your eyes off the action. This makes behaviour studies easier to record and less is left to memory. Data collected on tape can then be studied during the winter months when butterfly watching will be naturally restricted.

Should equipment for the recording and interpretation of ultrasonic sounds become as common as ordinary tape-recorders, we shall then be able to enter the world of butterfly sounds. Butterflies do make and probably receive ultra-sounds, and some also make audible clicks, rustles and a variety of small sounds whose meaning we can only guess at. The hibernating Peacock butterfly makes a sound when it is disturbed that could be described as rustling or hissing, and this is probably an additional means of frightening predators. The noise together with the flashing of the eyespot on the wings could easily scare away a mouse, for example, although this has yet to be actually observed. The tape-recorder then can work as an all-purpose field notebook which leaves one's eyes, if not one's hands, free.

What is the information that should be recorded? The first important note to make is the date, for this is important to understand the flight period of the adult, and also to establish the length of the complete life-cycle in the field. Many butterflies, for example, have more than one

Figure 54 Watch out for sexual and seasonal dimorphism in your butterflies. The male (left) and female (right) Gatekeeper demonstrate sexual dimorphism, that is differences in size and patterning between the sexes in a species.

brood or generation a year and in southern Europe they may have three or four generations. Sometimes these generations overlap and eggs, caterpillars, chrysalids and adults of the same species will be found in the field at the same time. Recording the date each time these observations are made will help to sort these generations out. In isolation the date does not mean much: the first day of May one year can be fine while in the next there may be snow and certainly no butterflies about, so always record the weather conditions at the same time (see below).

Dates of the first appearance of some of the butterflies in spring in northern Europe will vary widely, and when you see your first butterfly it is likely to be one of the species which hibernated in the adult stage for the winter. The dates vary because hibernating butterflies will venture out on the first warm day, which can be any time after New Year's Day, or even Christmas Day if it is sufficiently mild. The Peacock, Brimstone and Small Tortoiseshell are common butterflies which hibernate as adults. Sometimes the date on which a butterfly is seen can help in identification. For example, a yellow butterfly seen in early spring in Europe is most probably a Brimstone, and in Britain it certainly is, for no other yellow species appears this early.

It is useful to note down every occasion a particular species of butterfly is seen flying. The notebook entries can then be used to construct tables to show flight periods. For example, for the Green-veined White which overwinters as a chrysalis and has two broods a year, a typical year's observations might read:

Jan	Feb	Mar	Apr	May	June	July	Aug	Sep	Oct	Nov	Dec
o	o	o	o	√	√	o	√	√	o	o	o

while for the Brimstone, with one brood a year and the adult overwintering, the records might show:

Jan	Feb	Mar	Apr	May	June	July	Aug	Sep	Oct	Nov	Dec
o	√	√	√	√	o	o	√	√	√	o	√

(o absent √ present)

A hibernating adult Brimstone might be found in amongst the ivy in December, or tempted out over the snow if the sun is warm in January. From entries like these examples, the flight activity in the year shows up and the different periods of flight for the species becomes apparent. The further north you live in Europe or in Britain, the later will be your first sighting and the shorter the flight period. Further south, butterflies will appear earlier and will have more than one brood, but note that some may not fly during very dry weather. In the study of any species it is important to establish the number of broods a year; in a cooler year in northern Europe there may be less broods than in a warm year.

Another interesting feature to watch for in some species is the considerable variation between individuals of different broods (see figure 55). Sometimes broods are so different in colour and patterns that they were once described as separate species until their life-cycles were better known.

Figure 55 The spring (left) and summer (right) generations of the Holly Blue demonstrate seasonal dimorphism. The early generation lays its eggs on Holly and the later on Ivy.

In different years the seasons may be early or late and so the same stages in the life-cycle may take place on different dates from previous years. In this way the dates recorded can become a guide to the type of season enjoyed in a particular year. Even with variation in climatic factors, however, stages will occur at roughly similar times by mid-season in most years, and by the time the second brood is out, the dates will show little variation from other years. Each year has slight differences in its seasons and careful notes can reveal interesting short-term fluctuations both in times of appearance and in numbers of particular species. Over the years a fascinating picture can be built up of the effect of climate and local conditions on your own butterfly populations.

Another important piece of information to record is the time of day of the observation. Does the butterfly you are watching feed or fly (or do both) in the morning, or only in the later part of the day? Very little is known of the daily life of a butterfly and observations on one butterfly and its behaviour would be interesting and worthwhile. In colder weather butterflies will be active later in the day, and very often it is the air temperature rather than the time of day which is significant. In this respect the Postman butterfly of the West Indies has been studied in detail. The reaction of this butterfly to different colours was found to vary according to the time of day. In the morning these black and red butterflies responded to yellow and flew to yellow flowers to feed. By midday they were responding to red, one of the colours on their wings, and they were therefore attracted to one another and hence males to females. At this time the females are also attracted to red flowers on which they lay their eggs. Later on in the day the butterflies responded to yellow again and returned to seeking food before roosting for the night. Clearly the time of day could be significant when interpreting a particular behavioural response, as long as other factors are also taken into account.

One of these other factors to note should always be the weather. Sunshine and warmth, for example, are the ideal conditions for flight; warmth is necessary to raise the body temperature, and so warm sunshine finds butterflies far more active than on an overcast day. It is worth looking out for those butterflies which are so sensitive to sunlight that they settle as soon as the sun is covered by clouds. Strong winds stop butterflies from flying but even on quite blustery days there may be a sheltered side to a hedgerow where they can fly quite safely. Heavy rain sends most butterflies to their roosts but there are some that seem oblivious to it. Perhaps the need to feed is a stronger stimulus than the discomfort of a buffeting from rain drops. Few observations have been made to establish if humidity affects insects enough to stop them flying; you will soon find, however, that still, warm, dry and sunny days are when you will see most butterflies in flight.

Always record both the habitat and the locality in which the butterfly is seen, for this may also give a clue to its identity. This is more useful for butterflies with a preference for particular plants or with plant associations. Marshy areas, for example, may have different species in northern or southern Europe although certain widespread species which live in marshy areas will occur throughout. In Europe, the Lesser Marbled Fritillary and Frigga's Fritillary could be expected in marshy areas, the former in central and southern Europe, the latter in northern Europe. The Purple Hairstreak, whose caterpillars feed on Oak, will be expected in Oakwoods, whereas the Grayling will prefer drier, more open areas.

Noting down the surroundings and plant associations in which you see a particular butterfly will give some idea of the preferred habitat for that species, and noting where it is seen can help to build up a picture of its range. Much of our information on the distribution and habits of some butterflies has come from the diligent study of amateur butterfly enthusiasts. Migrant species may turn up anywhere but it is also true that even

Figure 56 Like birds, butterflies look for roosting places once the sun goes down. Many hide under leaves but others settle on stems and roost head downwards like these Common Blues.

the most sedentary species can sometimes be found in an unexpected habitat, perhaps just to confound the experts. A study of the localities in which your butterfly occurs can be considered at several levels. First is the range; this is the area over which it has been found, and marks the limit of its regular occurrence. Around the edges of the range, in the marginal areas, the butterfly may appear only in good seasons. The range can therefore be considered to be made up of the centre of distribution where the butterfly breeds and where it is found each year, and the edges or margins, where it spreads in perhaps warmer years. Both areas are dynamic and changing, particularly the margins, although the centre of distribution may also move as climatic changes occur.

Some British species are on the edge of their range in Europe. Their main distribution is in central and western Europe and only small populations on the edge of the range live in Britain. The Glanville Fritillary, for example, was widespread in Britain but is now restricted to the Isle of Wight. Until recently the Large Blue was another example but, in spite of careful protection in North Devon, it has now become extinct in Britain and its marginal range is reduced. The concept of the margins of the distribution of a butterfly has an important bearing on the conservation of rarer species. The butterfly on the edge of its range is less common by the very nature of it being in a fringe area, usually has smaller populations, and is very susceptible to climatic and other changes. In Britain such a butterfly can easily become extinct, particularly if it is fairly sedentary and not reinforced from the main continental population. It is important for conservationists to identify these factors, because it is fruitless spending large sums of money on the conservation of butterflies whose range is contracting naturally perhaps for climatic reasons. Detailed studies of butterflies and their fluctuations in numbers help to identify these factors. Many reference books and field guides give details of the ranges of butterflies, but these rarely indicate if a particular species is contracting, and they cannot give details of all the localities in which the species may or may not be found.

Care should be taken when the locality in which the butterfly is seen is noted; always remember that others reading your notes may not recognise the area from a local name. To be precise give the name of the nearest large town or geographic feature, or the map reference. Remember to indicate the county or district for problems can easily arise over many localities with the same name. There are over thirty 'Newtons', for example, in Britain, and writing 'Newton' Derbyshire, or 'Newton' Argyll, will help to locate the sighting more accurately. Remember also, however, that there may be two or more places with the same name even in one county. If you do not write this information against each entry in your notebook remember to note it somewhere with your observations. Even if you have no intention of publishing the notes, unpublished diaries and notebooks can be of tremendous value in the future to naturalists evaluating the changes in wildlife and in the environment. The popularity of old diaries and journals about the countryside increases every year, and since Gilbert White's *The Natural History of Selborne* (1789) many have been best sellers.

Finally, with the locality notes, record details of the geological nature of the area as well as its proximity to natural features like rivers or the sea, together with detailed information, if available, on the more precise local habitat. This is the habitat area which the butterfly population prefers. It may be a quarry, a stretch of hedgerow or a particular field; in its own way it is the home territory for the butterfly. The habitat preference for any particular species will be broadly similar over the whole of its distribution, but few things in nature are absolute, and in different areas

Figure 57 Bramble flowers attract a variety of butterfly species. A Small Copper is shown here, a Small Heath in figure 58, and White Admiral in figure 59, all enjoying the Bramble blossom.

the species may live in what appears to be an unlikely habitat. The Ringlet, for example, is generally a woodland or woodland-edge butterfly where it is seen along lanes and pathways, but in North Wales it flies over rough ground on a sea-cliff well away from trees. Never be too surprised at the sight of a butterfly away from its more usual habitat.

Look at and note the plants in the surrounding area when you see a butterfly. The close dependence of butterflies on plants, at all stages in their life-histories, has already been mentioned and for butterfly watchers the study of plants and butterflies together is a logical procedure. At which flower is the butterfly feeding? Which colour flower does it

Figure 58

prefer? Does it feed indiscriminately on flowers from different plant families and on flowers of different shapes? Does the flower have a long corolla like Honeysuckle, or is it more open like a Michaelmas Daisy? Does the butterfly stay long at one flower and what are its reactions to other insects on the flower or approaching it? Does it react to other butterflies flying past? These are just some of the questions to ask yourself when watching a butterfly at a flower; the information provided by the answers will begin to show you patterns of behaviour in a particular species as your notes accumulate.

Figure 59

Figure 60 Butterflies can be drawn to pieces of coloured paper or cloth. Here a Scarce Swallowtail in Greece is attracted to the white of an English newspaper.

Do not forget the possibility that a particular butterfly will respond differently from others of the same species in a given situation. Although we do not credit butterflies with the ability to respond individually, any difference in behaviour which is seen should be noted. Reaction to other butterflies as they pass or settle nearby is significant. If you can recognise the sexes, and with practice and close observation this is possible for many species, note whether your butterfly is reacting to the presence of another of the same or the opposite sex. How does it behave near butterflies of other families? We know that butterflies recognise each other by sight and by scent (see page 96). Is the butterfly you are watching responding to another which is outside its line of vision? You may see what stimulated the first reaction. Some butterflies will swoop down to investigate a flash of colour. Collectors often take advantage of this and whirl round a piece of cloth on a string; not all butterflies react to this type of lure, however.

As a principle, no observation is too insignificant to be noted down; it may be the very feature which is the key to an unanswered question. Notice the places where butterflies rest at night and whether they roost in numbers or individually. How early in the afternoon do they start to find a roosting place? How early in the morning do they become active? You can find out whether it is light or warmth or both which affects them. Both must be important because if temperature is the main factor many butterflies would fly on warm nights. Many sit tight on cool days but do they then have to move as they become hungry? Roosting places can be discovered by watching butterflies in late afternoon as they look for suitable spots, perhaps under Ivy leaves or in bushes. Each place must offer protection not only from bad weather, but also from many night predators and small mammals in particular.

For many people butterfly photography supplements or takes over from sketching. Photographs of species at different times of the year can be used to study the variation of the local population and also provide a way of 'catching' a butterfly for subsequent identification. Sequences of behaviour, both with a still and a cine camera, are a challenging approach to the study. All the resulting pictures can be used to provide a greater insight into the lives of butterflies, and of course they are great fun to take. More information and practical advice on butterfly photography is given in the next chapter.

Counting

The numbers of butterflies seen may depend not only on all physical factors, but also on many special conditions to which the local population is subjected. Counts of butterflies in a particular area are a marvellous way of assessing the populations of particular species and following annual fluctuations. So often we say butterflies were much more common when we were young and sadly this may well be true; there are few actual counts of abundance recorded, however, and often these are merely references to exceptionally large swarms. Counting the numbers of a particular species within a few yards of the path along a favourite walk is one way to get some comparable data. Do not forget that the time of day, the weather, and all other factors already discussed, must be taken into account when these numbers are studied.

More scientific accounts have been carried out by catching, marking and releasing butterflies, and then determining how many marked

Figure 61 A Monarch butterfly displays the wing tag used in migration studies on this species in North America.

individuals are caught on a subsequent day. These are then given another mark and released. Further recaptures show how many butterflies stay in the same area and how many new ones come in, and a formula has been devised for estimating the total population based on the recapture rate. Quick-drying paints are used to mark the butterflies and a small tag on the wing has also been tried. A small, printed self-adhesive label, like a price tag, is sometimes used. This is bent around the front edge of the wing and stuck to the wing membrane on each side where a small patch of scales has been rubbed off by the thumb and forefinger. These tags have stayed on for weeks and the butterflies seem unaffected. In fact tags have been placed on butterflies with broken wings which could otherwise not fly properly. The tag along the front edge acts as a splint and specimens marked like this have been recovered over 100 miles from the release point. Tagging allows the behaviour and movement of individuals to be more easily studied, assuming of course that the procedure does not harm the insect. Long-range migration studies on Monarch butterflies have been carried out by tagging with numbers on the wings (see figure 61). These are specialised techniques, however, and cannot be recommended to the amateur butterfly enthusiast.

The counting method more suitable for those who want a more reliable numerical estimate of their butterfly populations, which can be compared between years, has been devised by scientists at the Institute of Terrestrial Ecology in the United Kingdom. Here a Butterfly Monitoring Scheme was started some years ago based on the counts of butterflies seen as one walks along a particular route. It is essential the route is walked once a week during the season, and all the butterflies within fixed limits are counted. To give comparable results this limit, which can be merely three metres on each side of the path, must be constant for the whole season. The actual width and route chosen depend on the observer, although certain suggestions are made by the organisers for anyone who wants to participate nationally in the scheme. The walk, or transect as it is called, is divided into sections up to fifteen in number. Each section can be of different lengths, but each must be kept constant throughout the season. The recorder walks along at an even pace, noting on a special card all the butterflies up to five metres ahead and between three and five metres, depending on the limits chosen, on either side. In effect you must create an imaginary box in which you are walking, and then record the butterflies which come into it. The season for butterfly monitoring runs from April until the end of September. If you wish to assist in the scheme the instructions are given in a booklet *Instructions for Recorders* obtainable from the Institute (see Appendix V). To participate in the national scheme requires a fairly regular walk but it will add interest to it, and the results you send in will form part of a wider study.

You may like to devise your own monitoring scheme based on this technique for your favourite walk. If you look back at your records after a few seasons you will soon see if any one butterfly was previously more, or less, common. With a standard technique accurate records and interesting comparisons can be made, which will be more useful than just noting 'Meadow Browns common'. It is not necessary to go out on the same day each week, but roughly comparable weather is useful, and any time from mid-morning to mid-afternoon can be compared. A walk along a short transect once an hour would provide interesting information on daily activity, but remember the part the weather may play when comparing results from different days.

There are a number of other methods you can use to measure abundance. Counts of the number of butterflies over a flowerbed, or on a walk in the park, may not be suitable for the national scheme, but they will give data which is comparable for your own use. You can use your camera to record the condition of the habitat and this will provide a visual means of comparing different years. Always bear in mind the limitations of the counting techniques used and the potential margin of error involved, but do not be put off by this if you want to devise your own scheme. Remember too that variation in the number of butterflies seen during your walk over a period may reflect not only the population changes, but also the availability of flowers for the adults or foodplants for the caterpillars. The data can be easily recorded on a series of charts which you can make for yourself based on those produced for the Butterfly Monitoring Scheme, but modified to suit your own requirements. Data on abundance can be collected for all your local species but you may prefer to study only one species in more detail. The scheme of counting can be as simple (or complicated) as you care to make it.

All these basic observations can be made on the common species in your area and a study of individual species over a number of years, with notes on numbers and movements, can be a fascinating pastime. Even with common species, results from two areas will not necessarily be the same and comparisons with other butterfly watchers' notebooks are always interesting. You will soon become an expert on the particular species in your own area.

Butterfly behaviour

I have pointed out the importance of recording certain basic information when we sit down to watch a single butterfly or a group, but what exactly should we look for? Initially perhaps it is the sheer beauty of the butterflies which catches our attention, and then we probably puzzle over the species identification. This is the stage when most people stop but this is when the really interesting observations can be made. What is the butterfly doing and why is it doing it? Years ago the idea that butterflies had patterns of behaviour seemed unlikely; in fact the very word 'butterfly' was to the Victorians a term essentially describing disorganised behaviour. Relatively few studies on living butterflies have already revealed that their behaviour and responses are rarely random but often very purposeful, although we have not yet been able to identify their purposes. Certain responses to food or the opposite sex are fairly obvious, and have been appreciated for some time, but there are other aspects of behaviour, like territory defence and display, which are less well known.

Studying the behaviour of butterflies can be fascinating and many aspects can be followed. It may be a record of the number of different species feeding at a particular flower in your garden, or merely the habits of a single species. Even the responses of butterflies to us as another animal and a potential danger to them can be interesting to study, and can be compared with their reaction to other animals. Do individual butterflies ever get used to us? After all, we are part of the butterfly's environment. Behavioural responses of butterflies are complex and little understood, and one reason for this is the lack of detailed observations on their behaviour in different circumstances. For birds this sort of information is provided by an army of birdwatchers, and perhaps in a few years butterfly watchers will provide similar information for butterflies.

The butterfly watcher should be alert to the type of response he is seeing. Butterflies have eyes which, like those of other insects, are particularly sensitive to movement (see page 21). As might be expected, stealth and patience are the first essentials of the watcher and slow, measured movements will allow a close approach. Unlike birds, butterflies are not particularly sensitive to bright clothing, but one of the more obvious precautions is to prevent one's shadow falling on the butterfly, for this will be easily detected. When butterflies are disturbed their reactions vary and sometimes this is the first clue to their identity. Some species fly off for a short distance and settle, while others soar up and leave the area. With experience the different patterns of disturbance behaviour will be recognised. There are evident levels of disturbance for sometimes the butterfly will move away slowly for a short distance, as if checking on the impending danger. It is important to understand the effect *you* have on a butterfly and to separate this from its reaction to the other animals in its environment.

Many butterflies have a favourite perch or flower to which they will try to return, even after considerable disturbance. Once this spot has been recognised wait patiently for the butterfly's return. Butterflies returning under these circumstances are usually less nervous and will settle closer to the observer. In hot, dry weather it is not uncommon for the butterfly to settle on the watcher's bare arm and attempt to sip skin perspiration (see figure 65). You will seldom get a better opportunity to study the live butterfly at close quarters, and of course it cannot hurt you.

There is no doubt that many butterflies, especially the males, have well-defined territories. The idea of territory as a factor in bird life has been

Figure 65 Neither tame nor fond of human company, this Chapman's Blue from southern Europe is searching for moisture and drinking the perspiration on the skin. It stayed close for some time, resting on hands and bare arms.

understood for years, and is widely known through many popular bird books like the classic *Life of the Robin* by David Lack. In butterflies much less is known of this aspect of behaviour and there is ample scope for observation here. For example, we know little of the size of the territory a butterfly will defend. The border between the territories of two butterflies is where one will give way to the other. The 'battles' between butterflies are generally very gentle affairs with just a brief chase and little physical contact. Both parties might well be damaged if collisions did occur and in any case butterflies do not readily spring to mind as symbols of strength and determination! How the boundary marking is done is not clear. There is possibly some obvious landmark like a hedge, but it seems equally likely that the territory is marked by scent. This is a feature well known in mammals, but it has only recently been shown to occur in some butterflies.

Some excellent work in Britain on the Speckled Wood butterfly has shown its territorial nature when defending patches of sunlight in a wood. Speckled Wood males settle in patches of sunlight where they are more likely to meet females which are also attracted to these spots. The male defends the territory against intruding males and the pattern of the 'attack' is fairly constant. The two males flutter upwards a short distance before the intruder flies off and the owner returns to his patch. In one experiment a second butterfly was introduced to the sunlit patch without the original 'owner' seeing it. When they met they fluttered up and up to a considerable height, as though unable to settle the argument, both

Figure 64 In the autumn the Michaelmas Daisy with its mass of flowers attracts many butterflies. It is a recommended plant for the butterfly gardener. Here a Red Admiral has been attracted to its blooms.

feeling they had a right to that particular spot. One eventually flew off. Under normal conditions, of course, this extreme 'battle' would not occur for it would be a waste of energy. The territory of the male is probably scent-marked; the intruding butterfly must recognise this so that it flies off when challenged. Intruders may also be discouraged by some aspect of display by the owners of the territory, like the threat postures of birds and mammals, but as yet we have not recognised the signs.

While I was watching Speckled Woods recently, a group of six were contesting a sunlit patch. They flew around in an up and down, follow-my-leader fashion which resembled a well-drilled dance routine. When they circled they moved into tight formation which looked like an animated crown. One would settle for a short while but then join in the dance. There was evidently a female leading a group of males and they followed her closely in line. I am not sure what was happening in the aerial ballet I watched, but it is possible that patch of sunlight had not been scent-marked, as patches must move with the movement of the sun.

Experiments with other butterflies have shown that territory marking does confer right of ownership. In an experiment a male butterfly of a species which marks its territory was released, and then recaptured before all the marking was complete. A second male was then released in the same area, and he too marked a territory. This evidently included part of the first male's area for when he was re-released the two battled one another for ownership of the overlapping area. Neither would yield as each regarded that spot as within its rightful territory. The experiment was repeated but this time the second butterfly was not released until the first had completed all its territorial markings. When finally released the interloper recognised the markings and the claim of the first butterfly on the complete area, and flew off when challenged. It is obviously not good for butterflies to batter away at one another in the wild. Survival in normal circumstances is difficult enough and so territorial behaviour acts like a safety valve to enable the intruder to retire gracefully from the encounter without damage.

In all the known cases of territorial behaviour in butterflies it is the male which marks the territory; we have few observations on the behaviour of the female. There is endless scope here for observations. Watch out for a small difference in pattern or perhaps a small tear in the wing which will enable an individual butterfly to be distinguished from others of its species. This will allow it to be recognised over a period of days so that its consistency in behaviour can be monitored. Close observation will help to establish whether a butterfly has its own territory or whether all individuals move with equal freedom over the area. There is some evidence that some species mark a different territory each day, or even at different times of the day. Some seem to defend their feeding sites as much or more than any particular territory. Many butterflies seem to be confined by hedges over which they could fly if pursued, but which seem somehow to restrict them. A Meadow Brown in a field will frequently fly all round it a little distance from the hedge, which it seems to use as a sort of marker. In the woods the Speckled Woods have favourite rides up and down which they fly. Even on relatively open moorland, butterflies like the Small Heath seem to keep within an area, although there may appear to be miles more of suitable country. Watching would soon establish if there is a boundary or whether this is just an impression.

The territorial behaviour of the more colonial species, where a number of butterflies live in a restricted area, provides a contrast. In the Marsh Fritillary, for example, the populations tend to be isolated with small colonies in suitable damp meadows with Devil's-bit Scabious, the food-plant of the caterpillar, and usually a few trees nearby. In these local habitats Marsh Fritillaries may be quite common, and although they do wander to some extent, individuals usually keep to the colony's own territory. Here it seems that a population has a territory in which all individuals fly with no one butterfly owning any part of it – a sort of butterfly commune. The territorial requirements in a colonial species are not really understood and would benefit from more observation.

Watching the flight characteristics of butterflies forms part of studying most other aspects of their behaviour. Normal undisturbed flight is different from a butterfly in a hurry or being pursued. Similarly, flight during courtship, and flight patterns during a 'threat' behaviour to another butterfly over a territorial dispute, may be different in mode of wing beat and the aerial patterns performed, to normal flight. Sometimes the way a butterfly flies is sufficiently characteristic for it to be recognised without a closer look. The quick whirring flight of the skipper butterflies, for example, or the flapping and gliding of a White Admiral, are distinctive. Once the ordinary undisturbed flight pattern is recognised then various other forms of hovering or fluttering will be distinguished, and gradually we will understand more of their significance.

The idea of migration in birds is now readily accepted although in the eighteenth century it was hotly debated, with suggestions that Swallows might hibernate in the mud or even fly to the moon! Butterfly migration is now proven in many species, but the idea that these apparently delicate insects can undertake long journeys is still not widely appreciated. In the main, the long-distance movements, such as that of the Painted Lady from North Africa and southern Europe northwards in spring to the rest of Europe, are generally accomplished in stages. The butterflies breed on route and their progeny fly north as the spring advances. How far a particular individual flies from north Africa before it stops, and whether any actually fly all the way to Britain, has yet to be discovered. In some migratory species there is often certainly one generation on route through Europe, while others seem to be able to fly longer distances. Speed of flight, both in normal circumstances and on migration, is difficult to measure. Painted Lady butterflies have been recorded flying at between eight and fifteen kilometres per hour on migration. The eggs of some migrant females do not develop until after the migration, when their energy supplies can be replenished after the long journey. The 'decisions' to start and stop moving are aspects about which we know very little. Most of the studies on insect migration have been done on the locust, whose movements can cause great economic problems. For this insect there is an urgent need to understand the factors which initiate and terminate migration.

Migration in butterflies differs from that in birds in being one way only. The butterflies which reach us from the Continent do not fly back again, although there is some evidence for a small reverse migration by some of their offspring. Invasions of Britain by Large or Cabbage White butterflies takes place every year. These fly across the Channel and in some years when they are abundant, they come over in vast swarms. The spectacular migrations of the Monarch butterfly which moves across North America has now been well documented.

If you are lucky enough to witness butterflies on migration do not forget to record the time of day, the weather at the time of the observation and, if possible, for at least one day preceding it. The direction and speed of flight, wind direction and the general behaviour of the butterflies should be noted. Are they moving in a large swarm or small groups? Are the movements purposeful in one main direction or do the butterflies seem to drift past with groups heading in different directions? Is the migration of one species or are there several in the movement? If there is more than one how do their numbers compare? Coastal areas are often the places to see these movements but sometimes they continue far inland. In East Africa, where I have driven through drifting clouds of migrating butterflies, they present a spectacular sight. They also give rise to many local tales, the most accurate of which is that they bring cars to a halt by clogging up the radiator and causing the engine to boil! Apart from long-distance migrations there are many local movements. These are sometimes in numbers but more often involve just one or two individuals of the better-known migratory species, like the Painted Lady, moving through a district. Even some of our more sedentary species may have local dispersal movements, and these are always interesting to observe and worth watching out for.

Courtship, mating and egg-laying

Many studies have been made of the butterfly courtship displays which lead to mating, and flight displays are only part of this complicated procedure. During the courtship display flight the butterflies release chemicals called pheromones, which act as stimulants to the behaviour of the opposite sex. Pheromones can be described as external chemical messengers which carry information about the condition of the butterfly. They are difficult to demonstrate but may be seen to be released in an undisturbed flight display by the raising of patches of scales, or the

Figure 66 Early in spring, after their winter hibernation, a male and female Brimstone display in their courtship flight.

deliberate extrusion of brushes of scales (see figure 11). The sequence in the display would be well worth noting if you see it. Does the female approach the male, or does he pester her until there is some response? Does the mated female reject the attentions of other males if they approach her? In some cases it is known that a male will produce a chemical which acts as a repellant to other males approaching the courting couple.

Much of the recognition of male and female is by pheromones, but some of it is also by specialised displays and behaviour. This may vary from a fairly brief encounter after which the male and female pair, to a prolonged and complicated display flight with the male fluttering round the female. Pairing cannot take place until the female settles. The male then grasps the tip of her abdomen with claspers, which are normally concealed inside the tip of his abdomen. Pairing takes place back-to-back with the butterflies facing in opposite directions (see figure 67). Once coupled the pair may fly in a rather clumsy fashion with one butterfly being passively carried. In some species the male carries the female like this, while in others the female carries the male.

In his book *Curious Naturalists* Dr Niko Tinbergen gives detailed accounts of the Grayling's courtship display. Dr Tinbergen, a professional

97

Figure 67 This 'two-headed butterfly' is actually a mating pair of Duke of Burgundy Fritillaries. Here the abdomens, joined at their tips, are obscured by the wings (see also figure 63).

zoologist, was able to study this over a period of several years with the help of his students. The male Grayling is smaller than the female and has a light-coloured band along the underside of the hindwing. The males took up regular observation posts on or just above the ground and flew up to inspect every butterfly that came past, returning if it was not a female Grayling. Female Graylings were followed. Sometimes the female flew away, but if she settled the male also settled nearby and walked towards her. The female responded in one of two ways; she either walked away, flapping her wings, in which case the male ignored her, or she sat motionless, whereupon the male performed a complicated display in front of her. The male approached the female, walking round her until they were face to face. Then with a jerky movement he raised and shook his folded wings, finally striking the female with them. The male then moved his wings back and rapidly opened and closed them along their front edges. All this time his antennae were at right-angles to his body and moving in circles or semi-circles. The female stretched her antennae towards his wings and after a period of wing fanning the male opened his wings, moved them forward, catching the female's antennae between them. Finally the male walked round the female to stand behind her and, bending his abdomen sideways, mated with her.

We have mentioned the importance of pheromones in courtship displays and Tinbergen's experiments show how they are actually used, with the female's antennae brought into contact with the scent scales on the male's wings. He discovered in the course of his experiments that the Grayling was also stimulated by a combination of scent and colour. This type of observation helps us to understand how the butterflies react to one another at this critical stage in their life-cycle, and also shows how much fascinating detail can be revealed by careful butterfly watching.

After mating the male flies off to find another female, but the female now searches for a plant on which to lay her eggs. It is interesting to note here that she is now responding to a different stimulus to the one which leads her to a flower to feed. In many cases the female is looking for a plant on which the caterpillar will feed, but how and where she lays her eggs depends on the species. Some butterflies lay their eggs at random, scattering them amongst the foodplants, and if the caterpillars can feed on grass, for example, then this is not unreasonable. The Marbled White lays eggs in this way and it does not present too many problems for the tiny caterpillars when they hatch, for they will feed on many different grasses. In most species the female is very careful in selecting the correct hostplant for her eggs, and glues them tightly on. It is an obvious advantage for the newly hatched caterpillar to have its foodplant close at hand. Many caterpillars eat the eggshell before going to feed on the plant. The shell not only supplies them with their first meal but also probably provides them with certain important nutrients. In some species, the young caterpillar prevented from eating its own eggshell may die, even if offered the correct foodplant. Butterflies may lay their eggs singly, like the Red Admiral, or in batches, like the Small Tortoiseshell. The detection of the hostplant by the female is often by its chemical nature. In some cases a female can be persuaded to lay her eggs on the wrong plant if it has been treated with a chemical extract from the correct plant. Observations on egg-laying and the female behaviour at this time should be carried out carefully so that she is not disturbed.

Feeding

Let us turn now to interesting aspects of butterfly feeding behaviour which are quite easy to note in the field. The adult butterfly usually feeds on a quite different plant from its caterpillar. There are exceptions, how-

Figure 68 Not all butterflies feed delicately on the nectar in flowers. Some are attracted to carrion and others will feed on the sap flow on damaged trees. In the autumn rotting fruit attracts some species and here a Red Admiral feeds on a soft apple.

Figure 69 Chalk-hill Blue butterflies are attracted to a damp patch on the ground. This behaviour is called 'mud-puddling' and many species obtain moisture and mineral salts in this way.

ever, like the Painted Lady, which may well feed on thistle flowers after laying its eggs singly on the thistle leaf. Observations are needed on the times of feeding, how long is actually spent feeding, and the plants on which butterflies feed. Some butterflies prefer to feed at the sap from a

Figure 70 A Green-veined White feeds at a damp patch on the ground. This photograph clearly shows the shape of the forewing cell (see figure 12) and the way the veins in the hindwing are outlined, in this case with green scales from which the butterfly gets its name.

wound in a tree, some on ripe or over-ripe fruit, while others on carrion. The magnificent Purple Emperor is one of the species that will feed at rotting carcasses, which are often used by collectors to tempt this butterfly down from high up in the trees where it normally flies. In the warmer parts of Europe, and particularly in the Alps, butterflies are attracted to damp patches on the ground or to the banks of streams where blues, whites and skippers may congregate to 'mud puddle' in large numbers. A place may be attractive to butterflies because a particular mineral occurs in the moisture there, and it serves as a kind of butterfly salt-lick. Note the sex of the butterflies at these patches for they are usually males. It has been suggested that the greater activity of the males in the sun makes them thirstier than the females, and they need a drink more often, a suggestion that can only have been made by a man! How do you tell if a butterfly is feeding? The simplest way is to watch the proboscis uncoil and probe into the flower or liquid, and you will often see the pulsation of the body as it drinks. Most butterflies drink nectar in flowers and the length of the proboscis determines the type of flower they approach. The proboscis is usually of a medium length sufficient to reach into most flowers, but not those with extra long corollas like the Honeysuckle. Some butterflies are quite happy to share a flower head like Buddleia with other butterflies, but a few species seem aggressive and will chase off others so that they can feed in solitary state. Watch out for these differences in behaviour. It is surprising that relatively little is known about the feeding preferences and behaviour of butterflies in spite of these characteristics being so easy to observe.

Survival

With the onset of the cold weather in autumn, adult butterflies become inactive and their body temperature drops. This means that not only is it impossible for them to feed but they may well also freeze to death.

Figure 71 Small Tortoiseshell butterflies overwinter as adults. Here, two are hibernating indoors and are best left undisturbed. They will emerge on the first warm day of spring.

Peacocks, Brimstones and tortoiseshells nevertheless all overwinter as adult butterflies, and in the autumn they seek a dry sheltered spot under Ivy leaves or in sheds or houses (see figure 71). There they will remain, with their body temperature lower than usual and their metabolic rate consequently reduced, until the onset of warmer weather. Sometimes a warm day in December or January will tempt them out. They are unlikely to find any food at this time of the year, but it is not known if they then continue their hibernation successfully or whether they die off. More close butterfly watching is needed here. Ideally butterflies will not emerge from hibernation until the spring when Sallow (Pussy Willow) or Hazel catkins are open (see figure 62), and once active they look for plants not only for feeding but also for egg-laying. If you find a hibernating butterfly in the house do try to leave it alone. If it must be removed put it into a dry shed and not just out of doors where it will soon die.

Many species of butterfly overwinter in the chrysalis. The caterpillar of the Large or Cabbage White, for example, is fully fed by the autumn and pupates spending the entire winter in the chrysalis. In the High Brown Fritillary it is the eggs which survive the winter after being laid on Dog Violet in the summer. In the more southern part of its European range the caterpillars of this species may overwinter. The Speckled Wood is unusual in hibernating in either the caterpillar stage or the chrysalis all over Europe, when most other butterflies have only one stage resistant to the winter weather. Marsh Fritillary caterpillars live colonially in a web on their foodplant and in the autumn they strengthen this web or spin a stronger one, and stay quiescent all through the winter. They pupate in the warmer weather of the following spring, usually after feeding up again.

The signal which starts a butterfly's hibernation is not understood as some will hibernate even when the weather conditions appear to be ideal for them to continue feeding. It could be the shortening day which they notice. The Small Tortoiseshell, for example, often disappears in early August and although a few may still appear, many start the long winter rest in the warmest weather. In this species it is clearly not temperature which is stimulating the hibernation response, and any observations on factors which might cause this would be welcome. One theory suggests that the hibernation of the northern temperate butterflies is derived from the aestivating habit of their ancestors. Aestivation is the term used to describe the resting behaviour demonstrated by many butterflies in the warmer parts of Europe during very hot, dry spells.

The techniques used by butterflies to survive weather conditions like storms, strong winds and sudden night frosts, are also poorly understood and require more observations. Are butterflies killed by very heavy rainstorms for example? Certainly they are occasionally seen apparently drowned, but could they have died from the physical buffeting of the heavy rain drops? The survival of butterflies during their ordinary daily lives is another aspect of butterfly natural history to which the butterfly watcher can make a useful contribution. It has been estimated that a one-acre meadow in Sussex could hold two million spiders, not to mention hungry birds, mammals and other predators, and so it seems surprising that any butterflies do survive their daily hazards. Watching butterflies closely gives us an opportunity to study some real-life dramas for daily survival, and the means by which butterflies try to avoid or minimise these.

Techniques for survival are just as remarkable as many of the others in the animal kindgom. Like most insects, butterflies usually lay large numbers of eggs to compensate for the losses suffered during the vulnerable caterpillar stage in the life-cycle. The Large Tortoiseshell and the Peacock are among a number of species which lay their eggs in batches of 100 or more. The ability to fly in the adult is of course an excellent means of escape from attack from predators. Many species make use of their colours and patterns for survival. They are often camouflaged at rest, their colours blending with the background, or their shape is broken up by complicated patterns (see figures 47, 85). Most of these

Figure 72 Although quite conspicuous with its wings spread (see figure 75), at rest the irregular outline of the Comma camouflages it perfectly among dead leaves.

patterns are on the underside, for many butterflies close their wings when at rest on the ground or on bushes. The effect of wing closure can be dramatic. At one moment there is a colourful butterfly and at the next it has vanished; to a pursuing bird this must be most disconcerting. In his studies of the behaviour of the Grayling to which we referred earlier, Dr Tinbergen gave this butterfly a pet name, 'The bark with wings'. He describes how insects were congregating around the sap oozing from a tree. A Camberwell Beauty approached (upwind he comments, following the smell of the sap):

'... a small piece of the tree's bark detached itself from the tree, shot through the air towards the butterfly, whirled around it for a few seconds, then abandoned it again, and dropped to the ground, where it vanished as suddenly as it had appeared. Cautiously approaching the spot where I had seen it hit the ground, I failed to see anything until a small piece of dirt leapt into the air and dashed past me, back to the tree, where it disappeared at once reaching the bark. This was the Grayling butterfly or "bark with wings", as we called it.'

The Grayling is wonderfully camouflaged but it also shows a fascinating aspect of survival behaviour to make itself even less conspicuous when at rest. Alighting on the ground it will close its wings, withdraw the forewing behind the hindwing so that the eyespot is hidden and lean over towards the sun to reduce its shadow (see figure 73).

Figure 73 Even a well-camouflaged butterfly is vulnerable on the ground when its shadow can give away its position. On alighting the Grayling makes itself as inconspicuous as possible by retracting its forewing so that the eyespot is hidden, and leaning over to minimise its shadow.

Dr Tinbergen and his students made other experiments to test the various reactions of the Grayling to different stimuli. This species has a habit of pursuing other butterflies, dragonflies and sometimes even birds. The researchers made a series of cut-outs of different shapes and colours, and dangled these near resting Graylings to test their reactions. In most cases the Grayling flew up to investigate the shape. The research established that males were most responsive to dark colours, but that on the whole colour differences did not affect the response as much as they expected. Then the researchers discovered that if they added the scent of roses, lavender, or other flowers, the butterflies became more responsive to colours, particularly blues and yellows. This suggests a number of relatively simple experiments that can be carried out to investigate this type of behaviour, and which will not need a lot of apparatus. It is interesting to look at butterfly wing patterns to see which background they resemble, and to notice whether the butterfly tends to settle on this background. How do they know where to rest where they will blend with the surroundings? Presumably the most suitable resting site is chosen visually by the insect, but this is no less remarkable.

As day fliers, butterflies rest at night and part of the day on bushes or on the ground. Here they will be vulnerable to small mammals, but even against these they still have a trick or two. Watch a Peacock at rest, sometimes with its wings open but, especially towards evening, with the wings closed. The dark underside is not particularly conspicuous. When disturbed, the butterfly's first reaction is to open its wings rapidly, often making a faint rattling or hissing sound at the same time. On opening, the enormous eyespots on the wings suddenly flash into view (see figure 74). A small mammal or bird suddenly confronted by these large eyes is naturally deterred and usually moves off quickly. Dr Tinbergen gives some practical results from butterfly watching in an attempt to show whether eyespots really do frighten a predator. In one observation he

Figure 74 The sudden flashing of the Peacock's eyespots when it is disturbed is very effective in frightening off predators.

mentions presenting a Peacock to a Jay: 'The bird gave the insect a light peck, upon which the Peacock flapped its wings, scaring the wits out of the bird. The Jay jumped straight into the air, hitting the roof of the cage.' This was certainly a positive reaction to the butterfly and would have normally allowed it to escape. Confined to the cage, however, the butterfly was later eaten by the Jay which presumably was not to be tricked twice. The responses of birds and other predators to butterflies in the wild would make an excellent study for the patient observer, and offer a good example of the way in which birdwatching and butterfly watching can be combined to give information useful to both disciplines.

Many brightly coloured insects have distasteful chemicals in their bodies or they sting, making them unpleasant to predators. Birds and mammals soon learn to avoid yellow and black insects which might be wasps, and similar warning coloration can be important in advertising the fact that certain butterflies are not good to eat. This phenomenon, however, has led to a whole new means of defence for some insects, which might otherwise make a tasty meal for some predator. These insects have patterns and colours similar to distasteful species and so are also avoided by predators. The mimics, as they are called, have to be less common than the distasteful 'models' for the system might otherwise not work. If mimics are too common it might take too long for young birds to learn that some insects with that particular pattern are distasteful.

Observations on predators attacking butterflies are always interesting. Butterflies can often be seen with the marks of a bird's beak on the wings, showing that an unsuccessful attack has been made (see figure 49). Eye-spots may not only frighten a bird but also mislead it, causing it to peck at them instead of the body. They are then referred to as deflection spots. When butterflies are pursued by birds they adopt an irregular, evasive flight which makes them difficult to catch, even by specialist insect-eaters like flycatchers. A listener to the BBC wildlife programme *The Living World* recently sent me a good description of a Spotted Flycatcher's attempt to catch a white butterfly. Each time the bird attacked the butterfly the latter managed to avoid it and eventually it escaped altogether. A similar encounter was described to me by my colleague Bill Dolling. Here it was a House Sparrow, which is quite clumsy in flight compared with a flycatcher, in pursuit of a white butterfly. The House Sparrow seemed unable to predict the position of the butterfly each time it lunged at it in flight. The zig-zag escape flight certainly saved these two butterflies and is worth watching out for in other species. It is interesting to note that both these accounts refer to white butterflies which are very conspicuous in flight. They have a curiously jerky action and so must be even harder to catch when being chased. Direct avoidance behaviour by butterflies is unusual, but there is a species of South African satyrid butterfly which will dive into the bushes to escape when threatened. Evasive flight is more common and information on how these attacks are made, and by which birds, is always needed. Only careful watching will show whether there is a long aerial pursuit, or whether the butterfly is perhaps caught by one wing to eventually escape.

We have already mentioned birds and small mammals as butterfly predators, but butterflies are also eaten by frogs and toads and even fish, which have been seen to take them from the surface of water. Among the invertebrate animals, spiders are the most common predators. It is worth watching for butterflies caught by spiders, which if distasteful often adopt the trick of staying quite still. The spider begins to inject its venom but if it dislikes the taste of the butterfly it will cut it out of the web, or in the case of the Wolf Spider which jumps out of hiding on to its prey, simply release it. If the butterfly struggles the spider might well bite a few times before realising its prey is unsuitable, by which time the venom may have already taken effect. You might more easily notice the small red mites, related to spiders, which seem to favour particular butterfly species, although they do not usually kill their host (see figure 50).

Many insects also feed on butterflies. Robber flies (family Asilidae) are predatory with rapid and manoeuvrable flight and have little difficulty in catching butterflies. Dragonflies also catch them in flight and even beetles take their toll, usually by surprising them at rest. One of the most powerful predators of butterflies, however, are the wasps. Wasps are very active in hunting food for their larvae and in fact kill many harmful species of insects as well as butterflies. They will even take the powerful fliers like the Red Admiral.

It would be a very interesting project to note every way in which butterflies protect themselves from predation, and to try to identify all the main predators. Alternatively a study of an entire life-history, looking at the way each stage manages to survive, would be equally fascinating.

Variation in butterfly populations

One of the most remarkable features of animal life is the apparent repetition of shape, colour and pattern over many generations. We now know more about how this is achieved and the mechanisms of genetic inheritance are widely studied. Specimens collected by the Swedish naturalist Linnaeus in the early eighteenth century are still in existence, and some of his collection is kept in a special vault in the basement of Burlington House in London. Looking at these butterflies, which were alive over 200 years ago, one is struck by the fact that the patterns and the colours, which in many cases have not faded, still match those of the butterflies flying today. It is true that in most cases the next generation of butterflies is like its parent, but there are always exceptions and these are called variations. These are highly prized by collectors and whole books have been devoted to the variations and aberrations of an individual species.

Within a particular species of butterfly which may occur over a large area of Europe, small local populations may develop in response to some factor of climate, local vegetation, or just sheer isolation from the inflow of specimens from neighbouring populations. The isolated population may differ slightly from the others; for example, individuals might have a few more spots or a slightly different colour, and if this is maintained over several generations butterflies in this population will be considered a

Figure 75 The rich upperside colour of the Comma is in strong contrast to the well-camouflaged underside (see figure 72).

subspecies or local race. The local subspecies of the Grayling and Silver-studded Blue butterflies, which live on the Great Orme's Head in North Wales, not only differ slightly in size but also emerge several weeks earlier than the more widespread subspecies in neighbouring areas. Local populations which vary in this way are interesting to study. A reference collection of photographs of specimens taken in the same place over the years would enable certain aspects, like the frequency of the pattern of variation, to be followed. Carefully netted (see page 112) the butterflies can be examined, notes taken and then released. Are the variations in the population you are studying more common in some years? Is there any factor which you can correlate with this? In some species there is more variation in one sex than in another. The Silver-washed Fritillary, for example, has a greenish form var. *valesina*, called the Greenish Silver-washed Fritillary. This is often more common in the spring brood and only occurs in the female which is then referred to as 'dimorphic', occurring in two forms.

Figure 76 The delicate pale silver underside of the hindwings give the Silver-washed Fritillary its name. This is a true woodland butterfly which lays its eggs on the trunks of trees.

6 A closer look

The basic principles of watching butterflies in the field and recording observations have been covered. Now we will consider how we can get an even better look at the butterflies. It is easy, for example, for the bird-watcher to turn his or her binoculars on to butterflies. Since you can generally get closer to butterflies than to birds, the problem becomes one of how close you can focus your binoculars. Most binoculars will focus down to between five and nine metres and so the image of butterflies closer than this will be blurred. The older field-glasses, without prisms, will focus much closer, to within three or four metres, while even the small opera glasses with relatively low magnification can be used providing they focus on objects close to.

I find that my 10 × 50 binoculars (a magnification of × 10 and a 50 millimetre diameter to the objective or front lens) are quite suitable for watching butterflies, and that finding and following them with binoculars requires only the same skills used for birdwatching. There are some butterflies, however, like fritillaries, which are very difficult to follow in flight, but this can nevertheless be an entertaining challenge. Binoculars are useful for watching the interesting events on a flower head at a distance, even if you are unable to identify the species involved. There is often a tremendous amount of activity by all sorts of insects to be seen, and this can provide interesting viewing without disturbance. You can also use a telescope to watch a butterfly in close-up at rest on a flower head. Telescopes are more difficult to operate and will not focus on very close objects, but they have a very useful high magnification. With a tripod the telescope can be set up, focused on a particular flower, and the associated insect activity studied at leisure. For this butterfly watching I use my 25–60 × 60 telescope (a zoom magnification of × 25 to × 60 and a 60 millimetre diameter to the objective lens).

Neither binoculars nor telescope are essential for watching butterflies for with patience and stealth you can get close enough for some worth-while watching. You need patience to watch a series of events in the

Figure 77 A Small Skipper in characteristic resting position with fore- and hindwings at different angles, feeding on a species of hawkbit.

Figure 78 Ragwort is common in fields and hedgerows and is popular with butterflies during the day and moths by night. Here there are Gatekeepers (one with a red mite) and a Ringlet. There are also several other insects, including a soldier beetle, a fly and a small parasitic wasp.

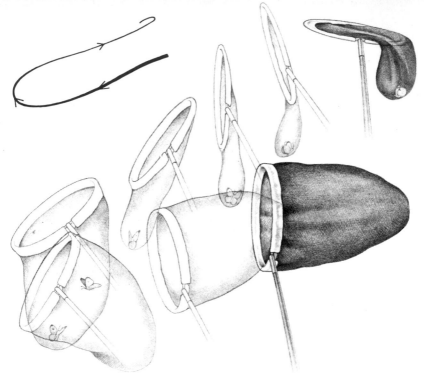

Figure 79 The final flick of the net at the end of the sweep traps the butterfly at the bottom of the net bag.

butterfly's life, and stealth to get a closer look at it. The need for a gentle but not necessarily silent approach has already been mentioned. When the favoured spot for a particular butterfly is found stand close to it, and the butterfly will soon accept you as part of the landscape. Half the fun of watching a butterfly is seeing how close you can get. When near look closely at the head and see if the proboscis is extended for feeding. Notice the details of the wing pattern and, when the butterfly finally flies off, the type of flight it has. With practice it will soon be possible to recognise this individual from further away, and this will help you watch its behaviour without disturbing it again.

Large magnifying glasses which have a long focal length and which will give a magnification of two to three times are very useful for examining butterflies closely. The small high-powered types are not so convenient because you have to get too close to your butterfly to get it in focus. They are useful, however, for noting the small differences between related species if specimens are in a net or jar.

For really close study and perhaps identification of some species, it may be necessary to catch butterflies with a net. Nets are generally made of a material fine enough not to injure the butterfly, and most are black

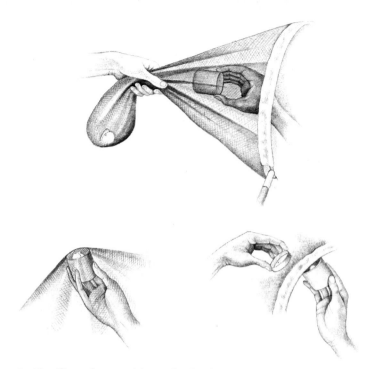

Figure 80 Handling of a netted butterfly should be kept to a minimum. If carefully transferred to a box or jar as shown here, it can be identified and released without even being touched.

or green and have a long bag. This is important for retaining the butterfly safely. Simple shrimping nets are not suitable and can damage the insect, which anyway will easily escape from the open end. Catching butterflies with a net is not as easy as it looks. A cautious approach and a swift final movement with a flick of the wrist to close the net bag is usually all that is needed (see figure 79). Some butterflies are easier to catch than others. Some can be caught by netting from the front, but others should be approached from behind; the most effective approach can only be learnt by practice. Everyone has their own technique; some enjoy the chase but personally I prefer to let the butterfly approach close enough before making a move! Netting rarely harms butterflies and they can be examined closely and released. To remove a butterfly safely from the net slip a small jar or box over it. The lid can be placed over the jar from outside the net, and then the net slid out from between the two without losing the butterfly.

Examine the butterfly with great care for the wings and the scales covering them are very vulnerable. If you have to hold the insect, do so gently on the thorax near the base of the wings, which will be folded over the body (see figure 82). The pressure here must not be too firm for butterflies can be killed by a pinch on the thorax. One of the best ways to examine a butterfly is to leave it in the jar, preferably with a twig or flower. It will quickly settle down especially if placed in the dark for a few minutes. With the temporary captive at rest you can quickly thumb through the field guide for comparisons with your specimen. Bird-watchers tend to frown on the use of field guides when actually watching a bird, and make notes for identification later on. With butterflies, however, it is very useful to actually use the guide in the field, for it will tell you exactly what to look for on the butterfly to identify the species.

Rearing butterflies

One way to get a really close look at not only the adults but also the preceding stages in the life-cycle is to rear butterflies at home. The mortality rate of butterflies reared in the relative safety of a cage is low when a few simple precautions are taken, and they can be released, perhaps after being persuaded to lay a few eggs, in your garden. It is possible to buy from dealers butterfly eggs, caterpillars, chrysalids and even the live butterflies themselves. Many people enjoy the fun of rearing butterflies, and especially some of the more exotic species. It is not a good idea, however, to release a foreign butterfly in your garden, or even a species that is restricted in distribution in Britain. There is a continuing debate on the ethics, desirability or disadvantages of introducing species into areas where they no longer occur, and generally this should be discouraged unless under the supervision of a scientific organisation like the Nature Conservancy. In any case such butterflies rarely survive long.

Some of our more common garden butterflies can be bought as chrysalids from dealers and allowed to hatch in the garden. Most popular are the Red Admiral, Small Tortoiseshell and Peacock. Providing the correct plants are present in your garden (see page 118 and figure 87) there is no harm in this, but remember the butterflies may not stay and you may be paying for extra attractions in your neighbour's garden! The technique to persuade butterflies to remain, apart from providing the flowers they prefer, is to let the chrysalids hatch in a cage in the garden. Keep the butterflies for a day or two with some flowers or sugar solution (see page 118) and when released they will regard your garden as their home territory, and there is more chance of them remaining.

Rearing butterflies from eggs or caterpillars is an absorbing pastime but there are a few simple pieces of apparatus, like cages (see figure 81), which are needed. The most important thing to remember is that once the eggs hatch, the caterpillars will need a continuous supply of fresh food. This can be supplied in three ways. The simplest method and the one needing least attention, is to sleeve the caterpillars on their foodplant. The caterpillars are placed on the appropriate foodplant growing in the garden, Nettle, for example, for tortoiseshell caterpillars. The plant is then covered with a fine net and the caterpillars left to develop undisturbed. Not all the plant needs to be covered, and the net with the cater-

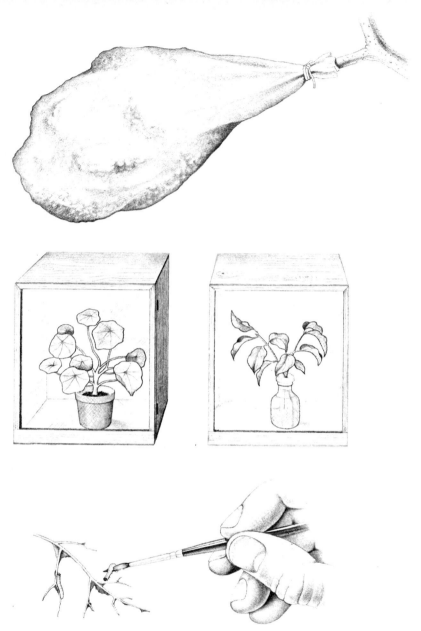

Figure 81 Sleeving (top) is the easiest way of confining caterpillars to a foodplant which is still growing. The sleeve can be tied at both ends to cover only part of a branch. Alternatively, cages are used to house pot-grown foodplants (centre left) or cut pieces in water (centre right). The cottonwool plug in the neck of the container prevents caterpillars from drowning. The easiest and safest way of transferring caterpillars from old to fresh food is by using a paintbrush (bottom).

pillars can be moved as the leaves are eaten. It is easier to sleeve the branch of a tree, and this can be done for caterpillars of the Purple Hairstreak and other tree- or bush-feeding species. It is better not to handle the caterpillars, particularly the smaller ones, and the best way of moving them to new leaves is to lift them gently with a fine paintbrush.

The second method of supplying fresh food is to keep the caterpillars on a foodplant which has been specially grown in a flowerpot. This needs forward planning to ensure that the plant is at the correct stage for the caterpillars, and that there are enough plants for them. The flowerpot is kept in a large cage and the plant left to grow naturally. The main problem with this, apart from preparing the plants in advance, is the quantity of food that just a few caterpillars will eat. They will soon strip a small plant and unless it is large, or there is a steady supply of small plants, it is difficult to keep up the supply. Most gardeners should be able to take this problem in their stride, but I think you will still be amazed at the appetite of small caterpillars!

The third method is more straightforward but the caterpillars will require a little more regular attention. Pieces of the correct foodplant are cut off and kept in an air-tight box; plastic ones are suitable, especially those of clear plastic which enable you to see what is happening inside. The box must be kept out of direct sunlight and the food renewed regularly because it will dry up or get attacked by moulds, which will be quickly fatal for the caterpillars. The caterpillars can be removed to the new foodplant using a fine paintbrush. Alternatively, put the new food in with the old and the caterpillars will very soon transfer themselves to the fresh supplies. Once all the caterpillars are on the new food the old remains must be removed, for hygiene is essential, even for caterpillars. Make sure the fresh food is not wet. Moulds rapidly develop in such conditions and other problems will arise. In a cage the cut pieces can be kept in water to keep them fresh longer, but the neck of the container must be sealed with cotton wool to prevent the caterpillars falling in and drowning. The caterpillars of some butterflies must be kept individually. Orange Tip caterpillars, for example, are cannibals and you may end up with only one, well-fed caterpillar if you try to rear several in the same container.

Many caterpillars can be collected in the wild, and this is probably the best and easiest way to start rearing them. Note the foodplant on which they are found and try to provide the same food. Some caterpillars will accept alternative foodplants, but others are very specific in their feeding habits and will eat only one plant. Searching the relevant hostplant for caterpillars is a slow but rewarding process, and it can be speeded up by using a beating tray or a sweep net. The former is a piece of cloth stretched over a frame which is either held under the bush to be beaten, or placed on the ground. A sharp tap on the bush will cause many insects to drop out, and the caterpillars can then be selected from the tray. Many caterpillars of moths will be obtained this way but it can be fun rearing any of them to see what finally emerges from the chrysalids. Beating trays can be made or bought from entomological suppliers. A sweep net is similar to a butterfly net but made of stout cloth. It is swept through the vegetation and many insects are collected. Anything may turn up (I have had a frog jump out on one occasion) so look carefully before you start searching in the net!

When the caterpillars are fully grown they will need somewhere to pupate. When this is about to happen they wander off the food supplies and may also darken in colour. They can pupate and form the chrysalis in the box or cage in which they were reared, but it is usually easier to transfer the fully grown caterpillars to a larger container. Place some sticks in this for them to crawl up and there they will attach themselves. Some caterpillars hibernate over the winter months and will stop feeding in the autumn, often staying quite still in the box. Leave them quietly in a cold but not damp place, and next spring watch for the first signs of renewed activity. Some of the caterpillars collected may pupate straight away, but most will want to feed up before forming the chrysalis. Give them fresh food and they will feed rapidly before pupating, often on the side of the cage but sometimes on the plants. If this happens leave the chrysalids on the plants unless they look as though they are going to rot. To avoid damage the general rule is not to touch chrysalids for three to five days after they are formed. Most butterflies pupate and form their chrysalids above the ground but a few, like the Grayling, prefer some light soil in which to pupate.

The chrysalids must be stored in a reasonably dry and cold place, especially those of species that normally overwinter in this stage. Others can be kept warmer to speed-up hatching, but they must be kept out of direct sunlight. Many butterfly breeders find that a very light spray of water just before the chrysalis is due to hatch will help the process. The chrysalis is ready to hatch when the wing colour and pattern appears through the thin skin. If you are in doubt that the chrysalis is still alive, be patient and do not touch it. In time it will become obvious it is not going to hatch, especially if others formed at the same time have already produced butterflies. When picked up very gently and touched, usually on the abdomen (the pointed end), it will wriggle slightly if it is still alive. There is also the old dodge of touching the chrysalis with the tip of the tongue. If it feels cold it is still alive, if warm it is dead. In a dead chrysalis the decaying tissue inside produces heat. Personally I recommend patience! When the butterfly emerges it is important that it has the opportunity to climb up a twig, or the side of the cage, where it will need to spend some time expanding and drying its wings. For this reason, it is important not to keep the chrysalis in a small box. Emerging butterflies may not have enough space to expand their wings which will then harden in a crumpled state. There are few sorrier sights in nature than butterflies in this condition for their chances of survival are nil.

The first requirement of a newly emerged butterfly is food. Place a

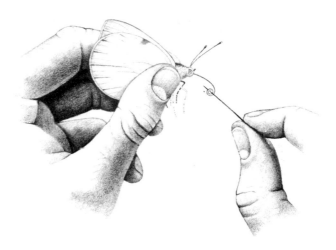

Figure 82 Butterflies will feed at sugar solutions but sometimes need persuading to start. With gentle handling (do not squeeze the butterfly) the proboscis can be uncoiled with a fine pin or needle and touched on to the sugar solution.

selection of cut flowers in the cage or provide a weak sugary solution, or honey dissolved in water (see below). Butterflies can detect sweet solutions through their feet and can be induced to uncoil the proboscis and start feeding by just touching their feet against the feeding liquid. They can also be persuaded to feed by gently uncoiling the proboscis using a pin inserted very carefully between the coils (see figure 82). Sometimes butterflies will not feed if they are too cold. With butterflies in captivity the difficulty here is that when warm enough to feed, they are usually warm enough for flight and become agitated. The best technique is to bring them into contact with the feeding fluid while they are still cold, and then allow the whole cage to warm up gradually out of direct sunlight. A suitable feeding solution recommended by L. Hugh Newman, one of our greatest experts on rearing butterflies, is half a teaspoonful of honey mixed with half a teaspoonful of castor sugar and a pinch of salt in one breakfast cup of water. Honey is a good food and the smell helps to attract butterflies. Do not make the solution too strong.

Release your butterflies in the garden on a warm sunny day so that they can continue feeding naturally. Many books will give more details on collecting and rearing butterflies, but it is not a difficult or complicated thing to do as generations of children who have successfully used jam-jars can testify.

Butterflies in the garden

Butterflies can be encouraged to visit your garden if a feeding table is established for them. After all, the birds will probably have a table in the winter so why not adapt this for use by the butterflies in the summer, or devise your own method of feeding? The honey and water mixture mentioned can be provided in a shallow dish or on a pad or cotton wool on a dish. Try placing a drop of perfume, preferably a flower perfume, nearby. Providing it is not mixed with the food this will help attract butterflies, and also provides endless scope for experiments. Which is the most effective scent?

The butterflies on the bird-table in summer may attract the birds. They can usually take care of themselves but try not to make them sitting targets. If they are attacked try suspending small pieces of cottonwool soaked in the feeding solution from branches at different points in the garden. One of the problems in providing food in this way is to keep out unwanted insects; ants in particular will soon find the food and can be a nuisance. The feeding solution can be put in small tubes with cottonwool wicks attached to sticks and 'planted' among the flowers. A paper collar around the tube will enable the butterflies to get more of a grip. Blue or purple paper has been found to be particularly attractive to butterflies. These feeding tubes can also be positioned among the plants at various points in the garden where they can be watched. These and other useful suggestions are contained in L. Hugh Newman's book *Create a Butterfly Garden* which is now unfortunately out of print.

There is still a lot to be discovered about the garden flowers which are the most attractive to butterflies. These naturally differ according to the season and to some extent according to the locality. It is not known whether butterflies in different areas have developed different tastes, and research along these lines would provide an interesting joint venture between gardeners in different places.

The plants which are attractive to butterflies seem to be those which produce plenty of nectar, are scented, and have certain colours. One way to study this is to cut different flowers from the garden and stand them in water. Put them in groups of similar species of flowers and also in mixed groups, and see which ones attract the butterflies. You can do your own investigation of colour and scent preferences. Does the time of day or the season have any effect on their choice? Different combinations of colours can be offered; five red flowers and one white for example, against five white and one red. Are more butterflies of different species attracted to one group or the other? Are groups of flowers that are attractive in the sunlight equally attractive in the shade? Is there a particular time when one flower is more attractive? The state of the flower must also be considered. The possible lines of inquiry are endless and it is fun to see which colours or flowers attract your butterflies for the insects will certainly not always behave as the experts predict. Another advantage of conducting this type of butterfly watching experiment is that you need to be sitting comfortably to see what is happening . . .!

As a gardener it is important to consider another aspect of insect life, namely that of pest control. If you go too readily to the spray you will kill not only pests but also butterflies and other useful insects. This is a difficult problem and one which entomologists have been trying to solve for years. Biological control, that is letting the natural predators and parasites reduce numbers of a pest, is the best solution, but this is no comfort to someone whose roses are covered in greenfly, or whose Cabbage is fast disappearing into the jaws of hungry caterpillars. It is always said that a good gardener will encourage useful insects like lacewings, ladybirds and syrphid flies (there are many others), but how do you recognise the good from the bad? This is often difficult, and the problem is solved by a quick spray clearing the lot! Spraying, however, can create as many problems as it controls. We really do not know all the answers but there are a few simple precautions one can take. If you must spray with insecticides avoid those which are persistent for weeks and try to use those that quickly break down into harmless compounds in the soil. (A solution of water and detergent is an effective spray against greenfly and has no persistent effect.) Do not spray flowers for this can kill many bees as well as butterflies. When using an insecticide follow the manufacturer's instructions carefully and remember that the spray can drift a long way. Using twice the quantity recommended will not kill twice the number of pests, and may result in twice as much harm to useful species. Used as directed sprays can supplement the activities of predators and parasites, but true programmes of integrated control with the minimum of spraying are not with us yet.

A garden for butterflies has something in common with our idea of the old cottage garden with a riot of colour and sweet-scented flowers. Most of us try for something like this and aim for colour through the season. What then should be grown with butterflies in mind? First, avoid the double roses, double paeonies, gladioli and other flowers, which have been so improved that their attractiveness to butterflies has been reduced. Perhaps 'avoid' is too strong a word here, but if your garden is filled with this type of flower it will not attract many butterflies, and those it will pay only fleeting visits. If these are your favourite flowers mix them with others to obtain a blaze of colour as well as the butterflies.

Among the flowers suitable for butterflies are the marjorams and sweet-scented Verbena. In spring Polyanthus and Aubretia, and later on the Alyssum and Candytuft, will attract butterflies to the rockery. The early catkins of Hazel and Sallow attract the butterflies which have hibernated over winter, and as the season progresses Wallflowers will come into their own. Tall Phlox and Sweet William will add to the attractiveness of the garden as well as appealing to butterflies. Later in the summer it is difficult to beat the Ice Plant (*Sedum spectabile*) and Michaelmas Daisies. Many colourful shrubs will attract butterflies and Lilac and Hebe are recommended together with the butterfly flower *par excellence*, Buddleia. Valerian is very popular with butterflies and you may also find the Humming-bird Hawk moth hovering round this flower. Watch out for those flowers in parks, and other gardens, which attract butterflies, and arrange for seeds of cuttings to be added to your own garden. It is now possible to buy packets of flower seeds which are especially selected for a butterfly garden.

Leaving patches of wild flowers in the garden is another aspect of butterfly gardening which appeals to some. Birds-foot Trefoil or Kidney Vetch (if you are on chalk) will add a new dimension to the garden, and even the common knapweeds from the meadows can be encouraged. Do not dig out all the tall thistles or Ragwort with its mass of yellow flowers (see figure 78). All these flowers are very attractive, as are many of the so-called weeds. A weed, after all, is only a plant growing where it is not wanted. A small corner of Nettles will provide many colourful butterflies whose caterpillars will feed on this plant. Watch to see which wild flowers are attractive to butterflies and note these for addition to the garden. Do not uproot them but when the seeds form take a few for sowing at home. Remember your basic gardening principles and, for example, do not try to germinate the seeds of an acid-loving mountain plant in a chalk garden.

Photographing butterflies

Photographing butterflies wild and free is a natural extension of observing them in the field. Purists will argue that the only way to photograph butterflies is by stalking them flying freely in the wild. Adults are not only the most attractive stage of the life-history, but also the most active and so present most problems. Nonetheless, most people start by trying to photograph adults.

In this book, there are photographs of butterflies taken both wild and free outside, and under controlled conditions in the studio. One of the main problems of photographing wild specimens is that they often show wing damage, unless they are found soon after emergence; whereas a bred specimen photographed immediately after it emerges, will show the wing shape and patterning quite perfectly.

Cameras and camera supports

Most British butterflies have a wingspan of only 50 to 70 millimetres and so it is essential to photograph them at close range to ensure they are a reasonable size in the transparency or negative. A simple non-reflex camera (or any fixed-lens camera) can be used for close-up work by attaching a close-up (supplementary) lens to the front of the camera lens. Close-up lenses are available in different powers or dioptres, which enable different magnifications to be used. Cheap close-up lenses are a poor investment, since they will considerably reduce the quality of the image. Close-up lenses have the advantage that they do not reduce the amount of light reaching the film, so no adjustment of exposure (either shutter speed or f stop) is needed.

A non-reflex camera, however, presents two major limitations when used at close range for photographing active insects. Firstly, since the viewfinder is offset from the lens, the field of view seen by the photographer does not match the field of view taken by the camera lens. This discrepancy, which is known as parallax error, is much more noticeable when taking close-ups than landscapes. If the viewfinder is above the lens, the camera will need to be tilted upwards; if it lies to one side of the lens, it needs to be turned towards whichever side the viewfinder is placed, so that the subject is better framed. This correction needs to be done with care, and preferably with the camera mounted on a tripod.

The second limitation is the need to measure accurately the distance between the lens and the butterfly if a sharp focused image is to be achieved. It is quite impractical to set the camera up on a tripod and measure the distance with a tape measure – the butterfly will have flown long before an exposure can be made! Sharp close-ups can be taken using close-up lenses on a non-reflex camera by attaching two stiff wires or rods to the front of the camera. These project forward in front of the lens for the precise distance at which the camera is focused. Different length rods will, of course, have to be used for each close-up lens. If the tip of each rod is positioned so that it lies just outside the field of view, it will not appear in the photograph but will help to frame the picture and avoid parallax error. If the camera is carefully moved towards a butterfly feeding on a flower, the exposure can be made once the ends of the rods are in the same plane as the butterfly. Cameras which have a rangefinder system coupled to the lens-focusing mechanism will be more practical for taking larger butterflies. Twin lens reflex (TLR) cameras have two lenses – the upper one is used for viewing the subject, and the lower one for taking the picture. Once again, the problem of parallax error occurs at close range unless there is an automatic parallax correction built in. Even then, this is not entirely effective at extreme close-up range.

For the serious entomological photographer, the ideal camera is a single lens reflex (SLR) in which the image seen in the viewfinder is identical to that focused on the film plane via the single lens. SLR cameras which meter the light passing through the lens (TTL) allow for more rapid adjustments to be made to the exposure than is possible by using a separate light meter.

Another great advantage of the modern SLR camera design is the ability to interchange lenses of different focal lengths. When buying their first SLR camera, most people are persuaded to get a standard 50 mm lens for a 35 mm format camera. Although this lens can be used for close-up photography by attaching a close-up lens on the front of the lens, or by inserting extension tubes between the lens and the camera body, it is not ideal for the person who wants to concentrate on photographing butterflies in the field. A macro lens – with its own built-in extension – allows for a very quick adjustment to be made to the size of the image. Many more macro lenses are available with a focal length of 50 or 55 mm than 90 or 105 mm, but the latter are preferable for stalking insects in the field. A 90 mm macro lens has a larger working distance (lens to subject) for the same image size, and so compared to a 50 mm macro lens, it is not necessary to get in so close in order to fill the frame with the butterfly.

Extension tubes or rings can also be used with a macro lens for still greater magnifications. These are sold as a set of tubes of different lengths, the whole set usually giving a life-size (1 : 1) magnification with a standard 50 mm lens. The cheapest extension tubes will be non-automatic, which means that the lens diaphram has to be manually stopped down before the shutter is released. This is a great disadvantage when attempting to photograph living insects. With automatic tubes, however, the lens remains fully open and so the subject can be seen right up until the moment the exposure is made.

When the lens is extended away from the camera body by either

Figure 83 The versatile monopod camera support in use.

extension tubes or bellows, less light reaches the film and so an increase in exposure must be made. This is no problem with cameras having TTL metering, because the exposure is made directly through the camera (some models do require the lens to be stopped down to the selected aperture first). When using cameras without any metering system, a separate light reading must be taken and the exposure increase calculated from the exposure tables supplied with the extension tubes. The increase will vary depending on the amount of extension (in mm) and the focal length of the lens.

The serious plant or landscape photographer would not dream of venturing into the field without a tripod; yet a butterfly photographer will cover more ground much more quickly without one. If a tripod is to be an effective camera support it must be sturdy, which inevitably means it will be fairly heavy. Such tripods are most useful for photographing butterflies within close range of a vehicle at a site where they are known to congregate. A monopod is a much more versatile and lighter camera support. This single-legged support can be screwed into the camera base plate and carried with the camera ready to use at a moment's notice. Figure 83 shows one being used to photograph butterflies feeding on a Bramble bush. This model is easily extendable to a height ranging from 60 to 160 cm.

Field photography

Taking good photographs of butterflies in the wild is a time-consuming job. Even if the success rate for sharply focused images is low, great pleasure and satisfaction can be gained by observing the behaviour of butterflies, and this may be useful for anticipating their movements. A sunny day, which is also windy, is not ideal for photography, since the flight path of butterflies will be unpredictable. Even butterflies which are resting on vegetation will move out of focus as the wind moves the flower head or leaves on which they are resting. But on a sunny day without wind, there will be plenty of light for photography and many more butterflies on the wing. Butterflies will be less active and so easier to photograph early in the morning and on cool days, but there will be fewer of them about.

Do not be too ambitious when starting to photograph butterflies in the wild. A smaller, more sharply defined image – showing something of the natural habitat – will be preferable to a larger out-of-focus image. Later on, the aim may be to take photographs where the butterfly fills a reasonable part of the negative or transparency, with most, if not all, of the butterfly in focus. In a head-on view of a feeding butterfly, it is essential to have at least the head, antennae and front edge of the wings in focus. In a side view of a butterfly at rest or a dorsal view of one sunning itself, it should be possible to get the entire wing area sharply in focus – providing the camera is parallel to the butterfly.

Unless a picture is taken specifically to illustrate wing damage caused

Figure 84 A single flash produces harsh lighting with side shadow. A second flash mounted on a camera bracket as shown produces more even lighting.

by predator attack, only intact specimens should be photographed. The aim should be to photograph a particular species as soon as the adults begin to emerge. Butterflies are best stalked by first observing where they alight and for how long. It soon becomes obvious that some individuals will tolerate a closer approach than others. Once a butterfly has been disturbed, it may be even more wary. The best approach is to prefocus the camera and to move forward slowly but continuously, rather than in a series of abrupt starts and stops. Do not look through the viewfinder until you are certain the pathway is free of obstacles. Keep the butterfly in the viewfinder until the image is sharp (or the focusing rods are in line with the butterfly) and then release the shutter. The first shot may be taken at too great a distance from the butterfly, so if it has not flown, keep moving in and refocus the camera for a second. Remember that a hurried picture is unlikely to be a successful one. Even if the butterfly is in focus, the photograph can easily be ruined by unsightly backgrounds. Dried Bramble or bracken stems cutting across the frame can be very distracting, as can out-of-focus coloured flowers. It may seem surprising to recommend considering the part of the photograph behind the butterfly, but a subdued background can only enhance the picture. Patches of harsh sunlight and shadows jar the overall image. A lower camera viewpoint may help to isolate a butterfly on a flower spike above grasses, and make

Figure 85 A beautifully marked Glanville Fritillary which was raised in captivity from a caterpillar. In Britain this species is restricted to the Isle of Wight.

it stand out against the sky. Light and shadow is another effective technique – a sunlit butterfly will show up clearly against a background in shadow (see figure 58), or a silhouetted butterfly will be sharply defined by a sunny background.

Separation of the subject from the background can also be achieved by means of differential focus. When taking close-ups, the depth of field (the zone of sharp focus in front of and behind the plane on which the camera is focused) is quite small, so that if the background is a matter of several centimetres behind the butterfly, it will appear out of focus. The depth of field can be increased by stopping down the lens to a smaller aperture (for example, from f/8 to f/11) and for this reason, the aim should be not to use the lens at wide-open aperture.

Since the correct exposure is derived by using the right combination of shutter speed with lens aperture, some lenses have these two factors 'coupled'. Once the exposure has been determined and set, any change in the shutter speed will automatically bring about a change in the aperture. Permanently using a shutter speed of 1/125 or 1/250 second will not produce creative photographs. Remember also that if you use a colour film rated at 50 or 64 ASA, the depth of field will be limited with fast shutter speeds compared with slower speeds of say 1/60 or 1/30 second.

Electronic flash will help to ensure a sharp image, even with camera shake, as well as an increased depth of field. When stalking butterflies the easiest way to use flash is to have it mounted on a camera bracket. Many right-angle brackets are available for a single flash but unless a reflector is placed on the opposite side to the flash, it will produce harsh lighting with a strong side shadow. For this reason, I prefer to use two flashes mounted on a specially made 'boomerang' designed by an Australian photographer (see figure 84). Small electronic flashes are quite powerful enough for close-up work in the field. Notice how one flash is mounted at a higher level than the other. The flash leads are connected to the camera by using a twin flash adaptor in the X flash socket. Many modern cameras have only a single 'hot shoe' connection for use with a single flash. The use of a hot shoe/cold shoe attachment makes it possible to then use a two- or three-way adaptor for two or three flashes. When using electronic flash with a focal plane shutter set the shutter to the speed marked with a red spot or line. This is usually 1/60 or 1/125 second.

Determining the correct exposure when using flash for close-ups will have to be done on a trial and error basis. Keep careful notes of the film speed and magnification used, and the flash to subject distance. If these

Figure 86 The colourful Painted Lady is a common migrant butterfly, seen here on Marjoram. This is a powerful flier, and a regular summer visitor to Britain and northern Europe from further south. The caterpillars feed on thistle but the butterfly cannot survive our northern winter.

are kept constant for the trial and the aperture only is varied, a correct exposure will be found for your flash, film and particular lens for a given magnification.

Butterflies can be photographed feeding on flowers throughout the spring and summer months, although mid-summer is the best time for the largest variety of species on the wing. Butterflies alighting on a plant to feed or on moist ground to drink give the photographer a better chance of moving in close than at any other time. The structure of the flower as well as the amount of nectar present will determine how long a butterfly spends feeding on it. Buddleia is renowned for its appeal to butterflies. Each long spike is packed with tiny flowers which are laboriously probed with the long proboscis. Small Tortoiseshells and Peacocks may spend more than fifteen minutes feeding on one Buddleia spike, giving ample time for focusing the camera and taking several frames.

When using colour film, try to select butterflies and flowers which will do justice to it, for instance a Large or Cabbage White feeding on white Privet flowers will not be so striking as a Marbled White feeding on Greater Knapweed. With black-and-white films, contrast between the butterfly and the flower or background leaves is more important than the colours themselves. This is why lighting is so critical when working in monochrome. Bramble bushes also provide a valuable food source for butterflies, both from the flowers and the fruits. On a single bush, there may be as many as eight different species feeding at one time (see figures 57, 58, 59).

Muddy ponds or river banks in the summer are places where butterflies can be photographed as they settle to drink moisture (see figure 70). Damp muddy dips in woodland rides are also places where woodland butterflies, including White Admirals and Purple Emperors, come down to drink. Be careful to avoid sudden movements, including a hurried raising of the camera to the eye, since butterflies are more likely to be disturbed and fly off when drinking than they are when feeding on a good source of nectar. Butterflies can be attracted to a given spot by baiting. Rotten fruit is particularly effective for Red Admirals (see figure 68) and dung will bring down White Admirals and Purple Emperors. In dry summers water poured onto muddy patches where butterflies usually drink will soon attract them down. Baiting is a useful device for bringing butterflies to a particular site where your camera and tripod are already set up.

Once butterflies have been photographed at rest, feeding and drinking, the ultimate challenge is to photograph them in flight. This requires even more patience and a good quota of film for there is inevitably a high proportion of wasted, out-of-focus frames, and some with no butterflies at all! Flight photography in the field is not easy but can be best attempted by prefocusing on a butterfly as it feeds, and photograph-

Figure 87 Some of the garden flowers which will attract butterflies: **1** Buddleia; **2** Aubretia; **3** Thrift; **4** French Marigold; **5** Heliotrope; **6** Sweet William; **7** Alyssum; **8** Candytuft; **9** Michaelmas Daisy; **10** Primrose.

ing it as it flies away. Butterflies will beat their wings at a rate of eight to twelve beats per second, where one beat represents the complete cycle as the wings are moved up and down. This is, of course, a continuous movement and if sharp, unblurred images of butterflies in flight are required, a fast film (such as 200 ASA) and a fast shutter speed or a flash must be used. A slow shutter speed can sometimes be used to suggest movement by producing a blurred image of the wings, but this is not an easy or successful technique. The exciting part of flight photography is that the precise positioning of the wings is not known until the film has been processed. Indoor photography of flying butterflies is discussed on page 131.

The courtship pattern of butterflies varies from one species to another, and so it is essential to make field observations before attempting photography of this aspect of a butterfly's natural history. Once a pair start to spiral upwards, focusing the camera on them is well nigh impossible. An easier approach is to wait until a pair start fluttering downwards, especially if their movements become restricted by vegetation (see figure 66). A fast film or flash is again essential. After the courtship, mating takes place and this is a much easier activity to photograph without using fast films or flash, since the butterflies tend to alight for much longer periods than when they feed. Even if a pair does take off, they do not usually fly together for a long distance. Mating butterflies are best photographed side on, so that both sexes can be seen in profile (see figure 67).

Many insects, including butterflies, have evolved colours or patterns which make them blend in with their surroundings and thereby escape detection by predators. Recording this cryptic coloration by means of photography is best done in the field using natural lighting. Direct flashlight can so easily result in harsh, unnatural shadows which can only detract from an effective camouflage picture. Do not fill the frame with the insect, but try to show part of the surroundings with which it blends.

Indoor photography

Photographs of butterflies taken indoors can never supercede *in situ* pictures illustrating authentic butterfly behaviour in natural surroundings, but they can usefully supplement wild and free pictures. Since the lighting can be more carefully controlled indoors, and greater magnifications are possible, more emphasis can be placed on anatomical details. When photographing insects indoors, a kitchen table, a workbench or even a bench inside a caravan, are large enough to use as a work-top. What is more important is that the working area can be enclosed to prevent butterflies escaping outside or to another part of the house. Lighting indoors can either be by natural sunlight shining in through a window or by flash. Photofloods or any other continuous artificial light source are not recommended, because they give off too much heat and the butterflies tend to fly towards them.

Flash units can be supported by using either lighting stands on the floor, or clamp stands, or table-top tripods on the table. It has already been pointed out that a single flash results in harsh shadows, which will be eliminated by the use of two flashes. A third flash can be used to backlight a subject. The positioning of the light sources should ideally be selected for each subject and the visual effect of each set-up can be checked by attaching a small torch to the side of each flash gun. A ring flash is a light source encircling the lens which is specially designed for close-up photography. Using a ring flash is a quick way of obtaining indoor close-ups of active insects, but the frontal lighting provides no modelling.

In addition to lighting, the background also needs to be carefully selected for indoor photography so that the butterfly is photographed to best advantage. While plain coloured boards do not attempt to simulate natural surroundings they help to simplify a close-up photograph. Alternatively, natural vegetation is acceptable.

If you rear caterpillars at home in the way described earlier in the chapter, you will have ideal opportunities to photograph the emergence of an adult. If, as recommended, several twigs or stems of the foodplant are put into the breeding cage just before pupation, the caterpillars will crawl up and pupate near the top of the stems. They can then be removed and positioned for photography more easily than when they attach themselves to the lid of a breeding cage. When hatching takes place a series of photographs can be taken illustrating the way the butterfly bursts from the chrysalis and hangs down while its wings expand and harden.

Butterflies which have recently emerged can be transferred either to their foodplant or to a leafy branch for photography. If they persist in flying off the props, they should be boxed and put in a dark place until they settle down. A useful way of containing an active butterfly is to place a loose box (made by covering a wire framework on five sides with transparent cellophane) over it and the plant prop. Every time the butterfly settles on the inside of the loose box it is flicked off through the outside cellophane. Once it settles on the plant, the camera can be prefocused through the cellophane, before the box is removed and the photograph taken. This technique avoids repeated handling of a butterfly which sooner or later results in scales being rubbed off the wings and abdomen. Chilling or narcotising an active butterfly may seem to be an easy short cut to successful portrait photography. In practice this is not the case, since such insects often look moribund, with drooping antennae or legs not clinging to the vegetation.

As well as static portraits, pin-sharp pictures of butterflies in flight can be taken indoors. Such photography, however, requires a considerable amount of gadgetry and so brief mention of the technique used to obtain figures 7 and 8 will be made here. The camera is prefocused in front of a light-tripping beam, before a butterfly is released into an enclosed area. If the butterfly breaks the light beam, it takes its own photograph by activating a photo-electric cell, which triggers the camera shutter and fires three flashes. This kind of photography inevitably requires a great deal of time and patience, since there is a high proportion of wasted film when the butterfly breaks the beam triggering the camera outside the field of view.

Magnifications considerably greater than life-size are necessary for showing the shape and sculpturing as well as the density of butterfly eggs. These can be achieved either by using several sets of extension tubes with a 50 mm lens, or by using a bellows extension and a wide-angle lens reversed on the front of the bellows. A reversing ring allows a lens to be screwed back to front on to extension tubes or bellows. For example, a 190 cm bellows unit, used with a reversed 35 mm lens, will give a magnification of up to × 6.5. Figure 14 (right) was taken with flashlight using bellows and extension tubes on a Hasselblad, to achieve a magnification of × 5 on the negative. The photograph of the butterfly wing scales, however, resulted from much higher magnification obtained by using a microscope (see figure 11). Most 35 mm SLR cameras can be attached to a microscope by removing the camera lens and connecting the camera body to a microscope adaptor.

Photographic projects

When butterfly photography is first attempted, any good sharp picture will seem a bonus; later on, a clear objective will help to select subjects and thereby create a purposeful approach to photography. Although this book primarily covers adult butterflies, photographing complete life-cycles, through the egg, caterpillar, chrysalis to adult is an interesting and challenging approach, since it involves varying magnifications. A local site such as a woodland, meadow, or even a garden, could form the basis for a photographic record, month by month, of all the butterflies which inhabit it during a year. A more specialised project would be to photograph all the species which utilise one kind of foodplant. A real challenge would be to attempt to photograph all British butterflies in flight!

7 Butterfly conservation

The word 'conservation' has in some respects an unfortunate connotation in that it can imply a static, non-interference with the surroundings. This is really a contradiction of its true meaning for the whole of nature is in a state of continual change and our aim should be to prevent undue acceleration of this change. Man has always affected the rate at which changes take place in his surroundings, and he now has even greater power to do this. Conservationists should try to achieve a balance between human needs and those of the environment leading to an active, dynamic partnership between the two. For example, when areas are cut or drained for agricultural purposes careful planning should enable some parts to be left as wildlife refuges without materially increasing the cost. Similarly the building of houses can create gardens and hedges which can provide a haven for wildlife. Unfortunately, human needs and human greeds are sometimes hard to distinguish.

Education is one of the best long-term methods of conservation. If each generation is made more conscious of our environment then the principle of the conservation of the countryside will become a natural part of our heritage. It is important that the aims of conservation should not be confused in the public's mind with restriction of access. 'Nature Reserves – no entry' is just as annoying as 'Private – no entry'. Without clear explanations and publicity conservationists might be seen to be preserving land for the few at the expense of the many.

In the first instance, explanations must be given as to why conservation practices are required and the benefits that will result. Some of the battles between conservationists and developers in the past would never have occurred had the aims of conservation been more clearly understood. For some years at least, these confrontations are unfortunately bound to go on. Conservationists must be vociferous about a particular project if it is to be discussed. We cannot afford to let the planners say, 'Let us build an airport or power station here and afterwards we will discuss how to preserve the wildlife'. Conservation cannot wait until tomorrow. It is not even a question of deciding if people are more important than other animals or plants, for the situation cannot be regarded in such simplistic black-and-white terms.

The conservation of insects cannot have the same immediate appeal as that of the Giant Panda or seals. When you consider how many millions of pounds are spent in investing in new chemicals to kill insects, or how many scientists spend their working lives trying to devise methods of controlling their numbers, it seems odd to even mention insect conservation. In the case of butterflies, however, there is the appeal to our sense of beauty, and there is the less obvious factor that the loss or destruction of any part of nature often means that it is replaced by something else, perhaps less pleasant. In other words, the delicate balance of nature might be upset if butterflies disappeared.

The aims and reasons for the conservation of insects and the problems this entails are the same as for all animals. Conservationists frequently talk of preserving this or that species. This is certainly their immediate aim, but it can create a mistaken impression of simplicity. Let us imagine that all woodpeckers were protected by law and no shooting or trapping were allowed. This would seem to give absolute protection to the birds, but would this be so if we cut down, legally, all the trees? No amount of protection for woodpeckers would then save them from extinction. This may seem an extreme or unlikely event, but it highlights the fact that destruction of habitat is the fundamental problem of conservation. If you drain a marshland for agriculture, marshland insects and birds must leave. Other animals will come but they will be farmland species and will bring with them agricultural pests.

There is no simple solution. We cannot entirely halt progress or development but we can try to preserve parts of the environment, providing this is done in conjunction with a scientific study to determine why an animal or a plant is rare. A species which becomes increasingly rare in Britain because of gradual climatic change cannot be conserved here no matter how many flag-days we have for it. We may be able to make its disappearance less rapid by setting aside protected areas where it can survive, but we cannot stop its local extinction. It is important that the cause of its rarity is identified before money is spent on its conservation. There may well be other species more in need of protection because of a basic loss of habitat.

Among butterflies the Glanville Fritillary and Large Tortoiseshell are disappearing slowly from Britain, and barely surviving in the marginal part of their range. This natural contraction of range is occurring all over Europe as well. The British Large Copper became extinct in the middle of the last century. Its population size may have been brought to a dangerously low level by climatic changes and the drainage of the fens where it lived, and so two factors, a combination of the man-made and the natural, may have finally brought about its extinction.

The Large Blue, which has been protected by laws from collecting and subject to intense conservation activities, was officially declared extinct in Britain in 1979. Ecological studies undertaken over the last few years had shown how the populations could be maintained, but the discovery unfortunately came too late, when the numbers in the field were too low for the populations to survive. The Large Blue is becoming rarer in northern Europe and until the reason for its overall decline is identified, no amount of careful management will save it.

Populations of other butterflies fluctuate in size tremendously over the years. One of the classic cases is the Comma which once disappeared from many of its old haunts in Britain. Then it gradually became more common and more widespread over the next decades. The Black-veined White formerly bred in Britain, but is now a rare migrant. As it is a pest of fruit trees in parts of Europe this is probably a species we would not wish to encourage. Species which have local colonies such as the Marsh Fritillary, Adonis Blue and others, always present problems. It is all too easy to inadvertently destroy these restricted species by habitat destruction. In Europe the Apollo butterfly is protected by law. This is an attractive species popular with collectors and without protection it might disappear as a result of excessive collecting.

Mention of collectors inevitably leads to the pros and cons of collecting. Collecting common species has now been practiced for several centuries and little damage has been done to these butterflies. Heavy and indiscriminate collecting of rare and local species is to be deplored and is unnecessary. The butterfly caught in the wild is often damaged and the collector will want a perfect specimen for his collection. How much better it would be to rear the butterflies at home and release the surplus specimens in the correct area, so that both collectors and conservationists are satisfied.

A balanced approach to both conservation and collecting is needed. Hopefully the contribution that the butterfly watchers make to our understanding of these remarkable and beautiful creatures will stimulate our awareness of the importance of even small parts of our environment. Realisation will come that all plants and animals, and even insects less aesthetically attractive than butterflies, have an important part to play in nature and have, however indirectly, an effect on our lives.

Conservation in Britain is now undertaken on a large scale compared with some countries, but in proportion to our size and population it is still grossly under financed. On the wider European scale, the amount spent on the conservation of natural heritage for the future is an even smaller percentage of the gross expenditure. In Britain the Society for the Promotion of Nature Reserves was founded in 1912 to sponsor bodies to acquire land for reserves, and to collate information about them. Its aims also included the preservation for posterity of part of our flora and fauna and geographical features as national possessions, as well as encouraging and educating public opinion about natural history. The SPNR eventually assisted in- the formation of the Council for Nature. Later it was decided that separate County Naturalist Trusts were a more practical proposition, and the SPNR became the umbrella body for the County Trusts, called the Association of County Trusts. On an international scale, liason between naturalists in different countries is maintained through the International Union for the Conservation of Nature and National Resources. On the professional side in Britain, much of the research into

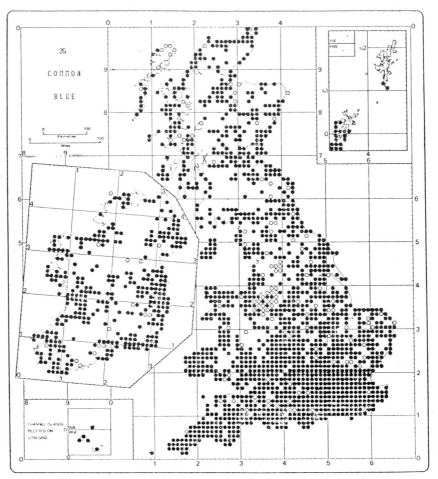

Figure 88 Distribution of the Common Blue. This map is an example of those produced by the Institute of Terrestrial Ecology in the National Mapping Scheme (see Appendix V). Black spots indicate sightings over the last ten years; open spots indicate pre-1960 records only.

aspects of conservation is done by the Nature Conservancy which was set up in 1948. Their work has developed over the years and has contributed a tremendous service to the countryside.

There are now many ways in which an individual can take part in conservation activities. The County Naturalist Trusts and the local Natural History Societies are the backbone of the system. Their addresses will be available in the local library. A committee of professional and amateur entomologists, the Joint Committee for the Conservation of British Insects, keeps a watching brief on the status of insects and makes recommendations to the Nature Conservancy for consideration and

136

possible action on conservation issues. Their aim is the protection of the fauna through voluntary means, but protection through conservation laws can be advised as a last resort. The British Butterfly Conservation Society (see Appendix V) was set up recently with the specific aims of protecting British butterflies. It encourages further scientific studies especially, with conservation in mind, and aims to arouse public interest in butterflies as well as working through educational establishments. The BBCS is currently promoting a habitat survey of British butterflies and provides information on the methods of conducting these surveys.

As your knowledge of butterflies increases you may like to take part in the national mapping scheme. This produces maps of the distribution of British butterflies and other insects and operates from the Institute of Terrestrial Ecology (see Appendix V). The maps produced at the Biological Records Centre (see figure 88) now provide the basic information for the study of butterfly distribution and they are updated every year. This splendid progressive scheme is always in need of people to supply information on the presence or absence of butterflies in their particular area. There are some parts of the country from which some common butterflies have not been recorded since 1960. This is not because there are strange gaps in the distribution of these butterflies, but because there is nobody recording in those areas. What is more, they are not all obscure, out of the way places.

Apart from local natural history societies there are three societies in Britain devoted to the study of insects. The Amateur Entomologist's Society and the British Entomological Society cater predominantly for the amateur, but also include many professional entomologists. The Royal Entomological Society of London is primarily a society for professional entomologists and is an international organisation with representatives in many countries. It takes an interest in all aspects of entomology. Addresses are given in Appendix V.

Appendix 1 The life-histories of some European butterflies

All the butterflies mentioned are found in Britain and continental Europe. The length of time that each stage of the life-cycle takes depends a great deal on temperature. The rate of growth of the caterpillar, however, will also depend on the condition of its foodplant; it will develop faster on a healthy growing plant. The length of an adult butterfly's life is difficult to estimate and needs more study of individual lives. In this list the lengths of the various stages are based on an average British summer temperature. The flight periods indicate the times when the adult butterfly is active.

Swallowtail
Distribution Throughout Europe but absent from Ireland and Scotland and only in the fens in Britain. **Life-cycle** One generation a year in Britain with sometimes a partial second brood; two generations in central and southern Europe with sometimes three broods. Eggs laid singly on Milk Parsley, Wild Carrot, Fennel and other related plants, although in Britain usually restricted to Fennel. Eggs hatch in 8 to 10 days, the caterpillar feeding on Milk Parsley and related plants. Fully grown in about 30 days before pupating. Unless overwintering chrysalids last about 20 days, although some remain over two winters. **Adult butterfly life** About 30 days. **Flight period** April to May; July to August.

Large or Cabbage White
Distribution A common resident but also a strong migrant moving into northern Europe including Britain in May, July and August. **Life-cycle** Usually two generations a year with a third in central and southern Europe. Eggs laid on cruciferous plants like Cabbage, Radish and Mustard in batches of 5 to 100. Eggs hatch in 5 to 20 days; caterpillars grow to full size in about 30 days. Chrysalids last about 12 days although second brood overwinters. **Adult butterfly life** About 24 days. **Flight period** April to May; July to August.

Small White
Distribution Large numbers sometimes arrive as migrants but also a common resident. **Life-cycle** Two or three generations a year in northern Europe, four further south. Eggs laid singly, one to a leaf on Cabbage, Mustard and other plants. Eggs hatch in 3 to 7 days; caterpillars pupate after about 20 days. Chrysalids last about 20 days excepting those which overwinter. **Adult butterfly life** About 20 days. **Flight period** March to October.

Green-veined White
Distribution A common resident but individually also flies in from the Continent in most years during the summer. **Life-cycle** Two generations a year,

three in central and southern Europe. Caterpillar feeds for 17 to 20 days before forming chrysalis. This lasts for 10 days in summer but overwinters for second autumn brood. **Adult butterfly life** 14 to 21 days. **Flight period** March to September.

Orange Tip

Distribution Resident throughout Europe although less common in Scotland and far north of Europe. **Life–cycle** One generation a year, rarely two. Eggs laid singly at base of flower or flower-stalk of Cuckoo Flower, Hedge Mustard and others. Eggs hatch in about a week; caterpillars feed on buds, leaves and flowers for about 25 days. Cannibalistic in early stages, they will eat any smaller Orange Tip caterpillar they encounter. Chrysalids last about a week. **Adult butterfly life** About 18 days. **Flight period** May to June in most years; can be recorded from April to September.

Clouded Yellow

Distribution Migrant in northern Europe including Britain where it cannot survive the winter. **Life–cycle** One generation a year in northern Europe; several through the year in warmer south. Migrants arrive in Britain from May to August (rarely April and sometimes September). Eggs laid singly on top of leaves of Clover, Lucerne and related plants. Caterpillars fully grown after about 31 days in northern summer. Chrysalids last 7 to 10 days. **Adult butterfly life** 25 or more days. **Flight period** April to October.

Brimstone

Distribution Resident in most of Europe including Britain. **Life–cycle** One generation a year. Eggs laid singly on underside of leaves of Alder Buckthorn or Buckthorn, hatching in 10 days. Caterpillar feeds for a month; chrysalids last about 14 days. **Adult butterfly life** Up to one year hibernating over winter. **Flight period** Frequently flies on warmer winter days. Normally seen June to July and in early spring about May.

Wood White

Distribution Throughout most of western, central and southern Europe into southern Norway and Sweden. In Britain and Ireland it occurs in south only including South Wales. **Life–cycle** Eggs laid singly on Bird's-foot Trefoil, Tuberous Pea, Bittervetch and other plants of pea family, hatching in 10 days. Caterpillar fully grown in about 30 days. Chrysalids last about a week; after summer generation chrysalis overwinters, the butterfly emerging in spring. **Adult butterfly life** About 14 days. **Flight period** May to June; July to August.

Peacock	**Distribution** Common European resident. **Life-cycle** One generation a year. Eggs laid in large untidy group on underside of leaves of Nettle. Eggs hatch in about 2 weeks. Caterpillars feed gregariously, living in a silken web which they spin as they feed (for 30 to 40 days before pupating); chrysalids last about 2 weeks. **Adult butterfly life** 10 to 12 months, hibernating in autumn and emerging in spring until May. **Flight period** July until autumn.
Comma	**Distribution** Local resident in Britain; has increased in numbers in the last thirty years; widespread in Europe to southern Scandinavia. **Life-cycle** Usually two generations a year with butterfly overwintering. Eggs laid singly on upperside of leaves of Nettle and sometimes other plants. Caterpillars feed for about 40 days. Chrysalids last for 10 to 20 days. **Adult butterfly life** At least 9 months hibernating over winter. **Flight period** June to late July; August.
Purple Emperor	**Distribution** Widespread but not very common in western and central Europe; very local in southern Britain. Does not occur in Scandinavia except as a rare migrant. **Life-cycle** One generation a year. Eggs laid singly on upper surface of Sallow or Willow leaves hatching in about 2 weeks. Caterpillar lives in a web hibernating after third instar (10 to 15 days). Hibernating caterpillar stays quite exposed over winter months attached to branch of Willow or Sallow; begins feeding in spring and pupates in late June or July. Chrysalids last about 2 weeks. **Adult butterfly life** 4 to 5 weeks, occasionally longer. **Flight period** July to August.
White Admiral	**Distribution** Local in southern England but more common in western, central and southern Europe. **Life-cycle** One generation a year. Eggs laid singly on upperside of Honeysuckle leaves hatching in about a week. Caterpillar hibernates after third instar over winter in specially constructed web and rolled-up leaf base. Caterpillar stage lasts about 10 months; chrysalids about 12 days. **Adult butterfly life** 25 days. **Flight period** June to July.
Red Admiral	**Distribution** Throughout Europe, but killed off by cold winters in the north including Britain. **Life-cycle** One or two generations a year in northern Europe, more in south. Eggs laid singly on Nettle, hatching in about a week. Caterpillar feeds on Nettle, living in a web which twists up the leaf. Each caterpillar feeds separately on its own leaf taking about 30 to 40 days to reach chrysalis stage. Chrysalids

last for 16 to 18 days. **Adult butterfly life** 1 or even 2 months before it is killed by the cold. Probably survives for 10 months or more in warmer parts. **Flight period** May to October; June to July and late summer in Britain.

Painted Lady

Distribution An immigrant in varying numbers to northern Europe, including Britain where it has become more common in some years. **Life-cycle** One generation in Britain and northern Europe, two in central Europe and more in southern Europe; a strong migrant. Eggs laid on upperside of thistles, hatching in about a week. Caterpillars are solitary, spinning silk over leaf and moving up as each leaf is eaten. Caterpillar stage lasts about 30 days and chrysalis about 2 weeks. **Adult butterfly life** Up to 2 months and probably more. Cannot survive northern winter; replaced each year by immigrants from south. **Flight period** April to autumn.

Small Tortoiseshell

Distribution Common resident in Europe; some migrate to Britain to increase resident population. **Life-cycle** Eggs laid on Nettle in a large group often piled up under leaves. Hatch in about 10 to 12 days. Caterpillars gregarious for first three instars, living in a web spun over leaves. If disturbed they jerk up heads and front part of their bodies in unison. In fourth instar (after third moult) they become solitary drawing leaf-edges together to form a 'nest'. Stay feeding for 20 to 30 days and remain in chrysalis for further 12 days. **Adult butterfly life** 6 to 10 months, and throughout winter in hibernation. **Flight period** March to October.

Large Tortoiseshell

Distribution Local woodland butterfly in Europe; formerly more common. Perhaps becoming rarer with destruction of Elm, one of its main foodplants, although it will feed on the more resistent Wych Elm, Sallow, Apple, Cherry and Pear. **Life-cycle** One generation a year. Eggs laid in a circle on Elm twigs high up the tree, hatching in about 3 weeks. Caterpillars feed mainly gregariously on Elm living under silken web for 30 to 40 days before dropping off tree and crawling up another to pupate high up. Chrysalids last about 2 weeks. **Adult butterfly life** 10 to 11 months, hibernating over winter. **Flight period** June to July; spring.

Dark Green Fritillary

Distribution Locally common throughout Europe; mainly non-migratory. **Life-cycle** One generation a year. Eggs laid singly on stems and leaves of Dog Violet, hatching in 14 to 18 days. Hibernate as soon as they hatch overwintering on Dog Violet. Feeding starts in spring, the caterpillar living about 10 to 11 months. Chrysalids last about 28 days. **Adult butterfly life** 20 to 35 days. **Flight period** June to July.

High Brown Fritillary

Distribution Throughout most of Europe; absent from northern Britain but extends well north into Norway and Sweden. **Life-cycle** One generation a year. Eggs laid on Violets where they remain unhatched all winter. Hatch after 8 to 9 months, the caterpillar feeding on Violets by day. Fully grown after 35 to 40 days; chrysalids last about 3 weeks. **Adult butterfly life** About 3 weeks. **Flight period** June to July.

Silver-washed Fritillary

Distribution Found throughout most of Europe; locally common in woods. **Life-cycle** One generation a year. Eggs laid on tree-trunks in woodlands, hatching in about 15 days. Hibernate in crevices on the bark over winter, climbing down to find their foodplant, Violet, in spring. Caterpillars live for 10 to 11 months; chrysalids last nearly 3 weeks. **Adult butterfly life** About 4 weeks. **Flight period** June to August.

Pearl-bordered Fritillary

Distribution Common throughout Europe. **Life-cycle** Two generations in southern Europe; only one in north including Britain. Eggs laid on Violet hatching in about 10 to 15 days. Caterpillar feeds on Violet by day until forth instar when it hibernates on underside of dead leaves, especially those of Violet, living for about 10 months before pupating. Chrysalids last about 9 days. **Adult butterfly life** About 10 to 25 days. **Flight period** April to May; July to August.

Small Pearl-bordered Fritillary

Distribution Widespread throughout northern, western and central Europe. **Life-cycle** Two generations in Europe; usually only one in Britain. Eggs laid singly on Violet, hatching in 10 to 12 days. Caterpillars feed under the leaves keeping out of sunlight unlike the related Pearl-bordered Fritillaries whose caterpillars seek it. Caterpillars hibernate in fourth instar, overwintering to start feeding on fresh growth on Violet in spring, and live for about 8 to 9 months. Chrysalis stage lasts about 2 weeks. **Adult butterfly life** 10 to 25 days. **Flight period** April to August.

Marsh Fritillary

Distribution Local over most of Europe in isolated colonies. **Life-cycle** One generation a year. Eggs laid in large masses on leaves of Scabious and hatch in about 20 days. Caterpillars live gregariously in a web on foodplant (usually Devil's-bit Scabious, but can also be other species of scabious and plantains). They will jerk up their heads in unison if disturbed. After third moult they spin an extra strong webbing nest, and hibernate over winter, spending some 10 months in caterpillar stage. Chrysalids last about 2 weeks. **Adult butterfly life** 2 to 3 weeks. **Flight period** May to June.

Glanville Fritillary

Distribution Local in western and central Europe; in Britain restricted to Isle of Wight. **Life-cycle** One generation in western Europe, including Britain; two in southern Europe. Eggs laid in large groups on plantains, hatching in about 3 weeks. Caterpillars live gregariously in a web on the leaves spinning a tougher silken web in which to overwinter. When alarmed they jerk up their heads in unison. When they start feeding in spring they tend to disperse from web. Chrysalids last about 3 weeks. **Adult butterfly life** About 3 weeks. **Flight period** May to June when single brooded; August to September.

Heath Fritillary

Distribution Locally common throughout Europe; in Britain restricted to southern England. **Life-cycle** Two generations a year in central and southern Europe; one in northern Europe and Britain. Eggs laid in large batches on leaves of Cow Wheat hatching in just over 2 weeks. Caterpillars feed gregariously under a web, hibernating over winter in fourth instar. If disturbed they jerk their heads up in unison. Caterpillars live for 10 months; chrysalids last for 15 days. **Adult butterfly life** 2 to 4 weeks. **Flight period** May to June; August to September.

Speckled Wood

Distribution Common in woodlands throughout Europe except northern Scandinavia and northern Scotland. **Life-cycle** Two generations a year in Britain and western Europe; one in northern Europe; several in southern Europe. Eggs laid singly on grasses, hatching in 10 days. Caterpillars feed at night on grasses for 30 days; chrysalids last for about 30 days. This species overwinters both as a caterpillar, living for 7 to 8 months before pupating, or as a chrysalis, lasting for 8 months. Spring brood butterflies are paler than those emerging later in the year. **Adult butterfly life** Up to 20 days. **Flight period** March to October.

Wall or Wall Brown

Distribution Common in western, central and southern Europe; does not occur in north of Scandinavia or Scotland. **Life-cycle** Two genera-

143

tions a year; three in southern Europe. Eggs laid singly on grasses, hatching in 10 days. Caterpillars feed on grass for about 35 days before pupating; chrysalis lasts 14 days. Overwintering occurs as caterpillars in which case this stage lasts for 8 to 9 months. **Adult butterfly life** Up to 20 days. **Flight period** March to September.

Grayling

Distribution Common throughout most of Europe as far north as southern Scandinavia but less common in central and northern Scotland. **Life-cycle** One generation a year. Eggs laid singly on grasses, hatching in 2 to 2½ weeks. Caterpillars generally pass winter in hibernation in second instar. Feeding recommences in spring and when fully grown caterpillar burrows 1 to 1·5 cm into soil spinning a lining of silk round the chamber in which it pupates. Chrysalis remains here for about 4 weeks. **Adult butterfly life** About 3 to 4 weeks. **Flight period** July to August.

Meadow Brown

Distribution Widespread and very common throughout most of Europe from southern Scandinavia southwards. **Life-cycle** One generation a year; caterpillar overwinters. Eggs laid singly on grasses and hatch over a long period after 2 to 3 weeks. Caterpillars feed on grasses on mild days in winter and live about 10 months. Chrysalids last 25 to 30 days. **Adult butterfly life** About 3 weeks. **Flight period** Butterfly flies even in dull weather. June to September.

Hedge Brown or Gatekeeper

Distribution Locally common throughout western Europe including Britain, but does not occur in north Scotland, northern Ireland or Scandinavia. **Life-cycle** One generation a year. Eggs laid singly on grasses hatching in about 3 weeks. Caterpillars feed on grasses, hibernating over winter when quite small. They begin feeding on grasses again in spring, eating by night. They live for about 10 months before spending a further 3 weeks as a chrysalis. **Adult butterfly life** 2 to 3 weeks. **Flight period** July to August.

Small Heath

Distribution Common and widespread throughout Europe. **Life-cycle** In south there are several generations each year; two in northern Europe and one with partial second generation in Britain. Eggs laid singly on grasses hatching in 2 weeks. Caterpillars spend 9 to 10 months developing, hibernating over winter in fourth instar to feed again in spring on fresh grasses. Chrysalids last about 25 days. **Adult butterfly life** 2 to 3 weeks. **Flight period** April to September.

Large Heath	**Distribution** Northern and central Europe; often rather local in mountain meadows. Does not occur in southern England. **Life-cycle** One generation a year. Eggs laid singly on Cotton Grass and White Beaked Sedge, hatching in 2 weeks. Caterpillars take about 10 months to develop fully. Chrysalids last about 3 weeks. **Adult butterfly life** 2 to 3 weeks. **Flight period** June to July.
Ringlet	**Distribution** Locally common in most of western and central Europe; extends into southern Scandinavia and as far south as central Italy, but barely reaches Spain; common in Scotland. **Life-cycle** Eggs scattered freely by female in grassy areas and dropped while in flight. Early instar caterpillars hibernate over winter, feeding again on grasses in spring. They live for about 10 months with a further 2 weeks in chrysalis. **Adult butterfly life** 2 to 3 weeks. **Flight period** June to July.
Marbled White	**Distribution** Locally common in western, central and southern Europe; occurs only in the more southern parts of England. **Life-cycle** One generation a year. Eggs scattered by female, often in flight and hatch in about 3 weeks. Caterpillars hibernate at once spending the winter in this early stage. In spring they feed on various grasses. After 10 months as caterpillars they remain in chrysalis for 2 to 3 weeks. **Adult butterfly life** 3 to 4 weeks. **Flight period** June to July.
Mountain Ringlet (sometimes called the Small Mountain Ringlet)	**Distribution** Lives in colonies in mountains of Europe; in Britain restricted to Lake District and Scotland; also reported from Ireland. **Life-cycle** One generation a year. Eggs laid singly on Mat Grass and other moorland grasses, hatching in 15 to 20 days. Caterpillars feed on mountain grasses, hibernating over winter until spring. They are said to feed at night. Caterpillars take about 10 months, including hibernation, to become fully developed and chrysalids last for another 3 weeks. **Adult butterfly life** 3 weeks. **Flight period** July.
Scotch Argus	**Distribution** Moorlands, mountains and mountain woodlands of northern England and central Europe including French Alps. **Life-cycle** One generation a year. Eggs laid singly on Purple Moor Grass and other mountain grasses hatching in about 16 days. Caterpillars hibernate over winter, feeding in autumn and spring on mountain grasses. They live for about 10 months and chrysalids last about 15 days. **Adult butterfly life** 3 weeks. **Flight period** August to September.

Duke of Burgundy's Fritillary

Distribution Local in western and central Europe but absent from Denmark and Scandinavia; in Britain occurs mainly in southern, central England and parts of Lancashire and Yorkshire. **Life-cycle** One generation a year. Eggs laid in small groups of up to 10 on underside of Primrose and Cowslip leaves, hatching in 2 weeks. Caterpillars feed by day for about 6 weeks. Chrysalis overwinters for about 9 to 10 months. **Adult butterfly life** About 2 weeks. **Flight period** May to June; August.

Common Blue

Distribution Widespread and common throughout Europe. **Life-cycle** Two generations a year. Eggs laid singly on upperside of leaves of Clover, Bird's-foot Trefoil, Black Medick and other plants of pea family hatching in just over a week. Caterpillars take about 45 days to become fully grown. Many spend longer feeding and hibernate over winter, living about 9 months until fully grown. Chrysalids last 2 weeks. **Adult butterfly life** 2 to 3 weeks. **Flight period** April to August.

Small or Little Blue

Distribution Widespread in Europe but not present in northern Scotland or central Scandinavia. Often lives in small, isolated colonies. **Life-cycle** Two generations a year in southern Europe; one in central and northern Europe, including Britain. Eggs laid singly in flowers of Kidney Vetch and other plants of pea family, hatching in one week. Caterpillars feed on the flowers and developing seed pods. If one encounters another Small Blue caterpillar on the same flower it will attack it and the stronger will eat the weaker. Caterpillar spins flowers together hibernating over winter in dead flower head, living for 10 months. Chrysalids last about 2 weeks. **Adult butterfly life** 2 weeks. **Flight period** June; August to September.

Chalk-hill Blue

Distribution Local on chalk hills and limestone areas in western, central and southern Europe. Does not occur in Scandinavia and in Britain limited to south of England. **Life-cycle** One generation a year. Eggs laid singly on Horshoe Vetch, but also on vegetation nearby which does not die down over winter. Eggs remain for about 9 months, hatching the following spring. Caterpillars crawl to the food-plant, Horseshoe Vetch, eating the leaves, mainly at night. They feed for about 9 weeks before pupating. Caterpillars often visited by ants which feed harmlessly on a secretion they produce. Chrysalids last about 4 weeks. **Adult butterfly life** 2 to 3 weeks. **Flight period** July to August.

Adonis Blue	**Distribution** Local in chalky and limestone areas in western, central and southern Europe. In Britain restricted to southern England. **Life-cycle** Two generations a year. Eggs laid singly on leaves of Horseshoe Vetch hatching in 3 to 5 weeks. Caterpillars feed by night on Horseshoe Vetch and other plants in pea family. Summer brood caterpillars live for about 2 months before pupating while late caterpillars overwinter taking 7 to 8 months to become fully grown. Chrysalids last 3 weeks. **Adult butterfly life** 2 to 3 weeks. **Flight period** May to June; July to September.
Silver-studded Blue	**Distribution** Locally common through western, central and much of northern Europe. Absent from Scotland and northern Scandinavia; found only in North and South Wales and southern England right up to Norfolk. **Life-cycle** Two generations in southern Europe; one in Northern Europe including Britain. Eggs laid singly on shoots of Gorse, Broom and other plants of pea family. Eggs do not hatch until spring, about 8 months after they have been laid. Caterpillars are fully grown in about 3 months. Chrysalids last 18 days. **Adult butterfly life** 3 weeks. **Flight period** May to August.
Holly Blue	**Distribution** Local throughout western, central and southern Europe. Only found in southern Norway, but occurs further north in Sweden; does not occur in Scotland. **Life-cycle** Two generations a year. Eggs of spring butterflies laid singly on flower heads of Holly, hatching in 7 days. Caterpillars feed on flowers, buds, leaves and unripe berries, and are fully grown in about 31 days. Chrysalids last about 18 days. Second brood lays eggs on flower buds of Ivy. Caterpillars feed up in 4 to 6 weeks before pupating, spending winter in chrysalis. **Adult butterfly life** 3 weeks and then cycle starts once again. **Flight period** April to May; July to September.
Brown Argus	**Distribution** Common throughout western, central and southern Europe; restricted to Wales and central and southern England. In the north replaced by the Northern Brown Argus. **Life-cycle** Two generations over most of Europe; three in southern Europe. Eggs laid singly under leaves of Rock Rose, Storksbill and related plants. Caterpillars feed on underside of leaves of these plants for about 40 days. In second brood young caterpillars overwinter, living for 9 to 10 months before pupating. Chrysalids last 2 weeks. **Adult butterfly life** 2 to 3 weeks. **Flight period** April to August.

Northern Brown Argus	There is some doubt over the relationship of this species to the continental Mountain Argus. The Northern Brown Argus is sometimes called the Scotch Argus but this confuses it with the satyrid butterfly of the same name. The Northern Brown Argus is currently considered a subspecies of the Brown Argus. **Distribution** Common in northern England and Scotland. **Life-cycle** One generation a year. Life-cycle and foodplants similar to previous species. **Flight period** June to July.

Large Blue	**Distribution** Local in western, central and southern Europe, into southern Sweden. Formerly widespread in Britain but has recently become extinct. **Life-cycle** One generation a year. Eggs laid singly on flower buds of Thyme, hatching in 7 to 10 days. Caterpillar a solitary feeder and should it meet another of its kind exhibits cannibalistic tendencies. After 3 weeks caterpillar leaves plant and wanders about on the ground. Eventually it is discovered by an ant which strokes it, stimulating it to produce a drop of sweet liquid from a gland. This is licked up by the ant and eventually the caterpillar distends the front three segments of its body. The ant then picks up the caterpillar in its jaws and carries it off to its nest (see figure 21). Here the caterpillar feeds on ant larvae and pupae for 5 to 6 weeks. It hibernates in the nest over winter, pupating in spring. Butterfly emerges after 21 days and crawls out of nest where it has spent some 10 months of its life-cycle. **Adult butterfly life** About 16 days. **Flight period** June and July.

Small Copper	**Distribution** Widespread and common over whole of Europe except extreme north of Scotland. **Life-cycle** Two generations a year in northern Europe; three further south. Eggs laid singly on underside of leaves of Water Dock. There may be several eggs under the same leaf. They hatch in 6 days and caterpillars feed on Sorrel and other related species. They eat grooves in leaf surface but later they eat right through. They feed for 3 weeks but in autumn caterpillars hibernate over winter and may live for 7 to 9 months. Chrysalids last 4 weeks. **Adult butterfly life** About 3 weeks. **Flight period** Late February to October.

Large Copper	**Distribution** Local in western and north central Europe with a small population in southern Europe. Drainage of swamps is causing numbers to decrease. British subspecies, which differed from European, is extinct although a continental subspecies introduced

into the fens of East Anglia in 1927 still survives. **Life-cycle** One generation a year. Eggs laid on Water Dock and hatch in about 14 days. Caterpillars feed on this and related species of dock, and over-winter on it living for about 10 months before pupating. Chrysalids last for about 2 weeks. **Adult butterfly life** Up to 3 weeks. **Flight period** June to July.

Green Hairstreak

Distribution Local thoughout Europe, except for extreme north of Scotland. **Life-cycle** One generation a year although a partial second has been reported. Eggs laid singly on flowers and shoots of Dyer's Greenweed, Broom, Gorse, Dogwood, Bird's-foot Trefoil and other plants, hatching in 8 days. Caterpillars feed on plants on which eggs laid but also cannibalistic. Caterpillars fully grown after 25 days; hibernate in chrysalis which lasts about 10 months. **Adult butterfly life** 2 to 4 weeks. **Flight period** March to June.

Brown Hairstreak

Distribution Locally common in western, central and southern Europe and into southern Sweden. Very local in central England; more widespread in southern England; local in western Ireland. **Life-cycle** One generation a year. Eggs laid singly on shoots of Blackthorn and Damson remaining there over winter and hatching the following spring after 8 to 9 months. Caterpillars feed on same plants and are fully grown in about 2½ months. Chrysalids last 3 to 4 weeks. **Adult butterfly life** 2 to 3 weeks. **Flight period** July to September.

Purple Hairstreak

Distribution Local throughout western, central and southern Europe into southern Scandinavia. Occurs locally throughout England and Wales and in a few localities in western Scotland; local in Ireland but few recent records. **Life-cycle** One generation a year. Eggs laid on twigs of Oak close to young buds. Eggs overwinter hatching after 8 to 9 months in following spring. Caterpillars feed on buds and young leaves of Oak living concealed under silk; fully grown after 6 weeks. Chrysalis forms on trunk of trees lasting for 36 days. **Adult butterfly life** Up to 4 weeks. **Flight period** July to September.

Black Hairstreak

Distribution Widespread but local in central and southern Europe; restricted in Britain to a few localities in the Midlands. **Life-cycle** One generation a year. Eggs laid singly on Blackthorn, sometimes on Plum, remaining without hatching until following spring. Caterpillars feed on Blackthorn especially on buds. Chrysalis formed after about 2 months and camouflaged to resemble bird droppings. Chrysalids last about $2\frac{1}{2}$ weeks. **Adult butterfly life** Up to 3 weeks. **Flight period** June to July.

White-letter Hairstreak

Distribution Local throughout western, central and southern Europe just into south Scandinavia; restricted in Britain and very local in central, southern, and south-west England. **Life-cycle** Eggs laid singly in forks of twigs of Elm and Lime where they spend the winter, hatching following spring after 8 to 9 months. Caterpillars feed on Elm, Lime and other trees; fully grown after 6 weeks. Chrysalids last 26 days. **Adult butterfly life** Up to 3 weeks. **Flight period** July to August.

Small Skipper

Distribution Throughout western, central and southern Europe including Denmark, central and southern England and Wales. **Life-cycle** One generation a year. Eggs laid in groups of 3 to 5 on grasses hatching in 3 weeks. Caterpillars eat eggshell on hatching and spin cocoon of silk inside leaf sheath where they hibernate for winter. Continue feeding in spring, tying together edges of a blade of grass to make a tube in which to live. After 10 to 11 months, during which they have overwintered, they spin together tube made of several blades of grass, pupating in this. Chrysalids last 2 to 3 weeks. **Adult butterfly life** Up to 20 days. **Flight period** June to August.

Essex Skipper

Distribution Common throughout western, central and southern Europe, extending into southern Scandinavia; very local in East Anglia and the Midlands, south east and southern England. **Life-cycle** One generation a year. Eggs laid in rows on leaf sheaths of grasses, hatching 8 to 9 months later the following spring. Caterpillars feed on grasses for about 60 days. Chrysalids last about 3 weeks. **Adult butterfly life** 18 to 20 days. **Flight period** June to August.

Lulworth Skipper

Distribution Local in central, southern and western Europe; does not occur in Scandinavia; restricted in Britain to a very small area in south of England. **Life-cycle** One generation a year. Eggs laid in rows on grass, hatching in 3 weeks. Caterpillars feed on grasses, spinning silken cocoon as soon as they hatch in which to overwinter. Pupate following spring; chrysalids last about 2 weeks. **Adult butterfly life** About 3 weeks. **Flight period** May to August.

Dingy Skipper

Distribution Common over most of western, central and southern Europe extending into southern

Scandinavia; common throughout England and Wales; local in Scotland and Ireland. **Life-cycle** Two generations a year in southern Europe, one in northern Europe and Britain, although sometimes a partial second brood. Eggs laid singly on leaves of Bird's-foot Trefoil and related plants of pea family hatching in 9 to 12 days. Caterpillars feed on leaves of Bird's-foot Trefoil and related plants, spinning a few leaves together and living inside the tent this forms. When fully grown they spin a tent-like cocoon where they hibernate over winter. Caterpillars pupate the following spring about 10 months after hatching and chrysalis forms inside this silk cocoon. Chrysalids last 35 days. **Adult butterfly life** About 18 days. **Flight period** May to June; August to September.

Grizzled Skipper

Distribution Local throughout western, central and southern Europe and into southern Scandinavia; locally common in central and southern England and into South Wales. **Life-cycle** Two generations in southern Europe, usually one in the north. Eggs laid singly on upper sides of Wild Strawberry, Silverweed, Bramble and other plants, hatching in 8 to 10 days. Caterpillars spin a web over midrib of leaves; later they roll leaf over and live in the tube formed. After 60 days they spin cocoon with leaves and silk on lower part of plants in which they pupate and overwinter, the butterfly emerging in spring. **Adult butterfly life** About 2 weeks. **Flight period** April to June; July to August.

Chequered Skipper

Distribution Locally common in western, central and northern Europe; in Britain local in Scotland (possibly extinct). **Life-cycle** One generation a year in the north, including Britain; two further south in Europe. Eggs laid singly on blades of grass hatching in 10 days. Caterpillars fasten edges of blades of grass together with silk to form a tube, feeding on grass below and above tube. In autumn they make longer tubes in which they hibernate, living for about 10 months before pupating in spring. Chrysalids last 6 weeks. **Adult butterfly life** 2 to 3 weeks. **Flight period** April to June; July to August.

Silver-spotted Skipper

Distribution Locally common over wide area of western, central and southern Europe and parts of Scandinavia; restricted to chalk areas of central southern and southern parts of England. **Life-cycle** One generation a year. Eggs laid singly on blades of grass and overwinter hatching the following spring. They are in the field for about 8 or 9 months. Caterpillars spin blades of grass together with silk to form a tent in which they live, feeding on the grasses. Pupate after about 100 days; chrysalids last about 10 days. **Adult butterfly life** 2 weeks. **Flight period** July to August.

Large Skipper

Distribution Widespread in Europe except for northern Scotland and northern Scandinavia; locally common in England and Wales. **Life-cycle** One generation a year in northern Europe; two in southern Europe. Eggs laid singly under blades of grass, hatching in 18 days. Caterpillars spin several blades to form tubes in which they live and feed. They make a stouter cocoon in which to pass winter, pupating following spring. Chrysalids last about 3 weeks. **Adult butterfly life** About 3 weeks. **Flight period** June to August.

Appendix II   Projects

Throughout this book there are many questions posed. Some idea of the present state of our knowledge of butterflies can be gained from the fact that the majority of these are unanswered. These questions can form the basis of projects and many have been referred to at various places in the text. For ease of reference they are grouped here in topics with page references.

Adult butterfly

Life-history

Appendix III Scientific names of butterflies mentioned in text

Adonis Blue   *Lysandra bellargus*
Alpine Grayling   *Oeneis glacialis*
Apollo   *Parnassius apollo*
Arctic Ringlet   *Erebia disa*
Bath White   *Pontia daplidice*
Black Hairstreak   *Strymonidia pruni*
Black-veined White   *Aporia crataegi*
Bog Fritillary   *Proclossiana eunomia*
Brimstone   *Gonepteryx rhamni*
British Large Copper
    Lycaena dispar dispar
Brown Argus   *Aricia agestis*
Brown Hairstreak   *Thecla betulae*
Cabbage White   *Pieris brassicae*
Camberwell Beauty
    Nymphalis antiopa
Cardinal   *Pandoriana pandora*
    formerly *Argynnis*
Chalk-hill Blue   *Lysandra coridon*
Chapman's Blue   *Plebicula thersites*
Chequered Skipper
    Carterocephalus palaemon
Clouded Yellow   *Colias croceus*
Comma   *Polygonia c-album*
Common Blue   *Polyommatus icarus*
Cranberry Fritillary
    Boloria aquilonaris
Cynthia's Fritillary
    Euphydryas cynthia
Damon Blue   *Agrodiaetus damon*
Dark Green Fritillary   *Argynnis aglaja*
Dingy Skipper   *Erynnis tages*
Duke of Burgundy's Fritillary
    Hamearis lucina
Dutch Large Copper
    Lycaena dispar batavus
Essex Skipper   *Thymelicus lineola*
Festoon   *Zerynthia polyxena*
Frejya's Fritillary   *Clossiana freija*
Frigga's Fritillary   *Clossiana frigga*
Gatekeeper   *Pyronia tithonus*
Glanville Fritillary   *Militaea cinxia*
Grayling   *Hipparchia semele*
Green Hairstreak   *Callophrys rubi*
Greenish Silver-washed Fritillary
    Argynnis paphia var. *valesina*
Green-veined White   *Pieris napi*

Grizzled Skipper   *Pyrgus malvae*
Heath Fritillary   *Mellicta athalia*
Hedge Brown   *Pyronia tithonus*
High Brown Fritillary   *Argynnis adippe*
Holly Blue   *Celastrina argiolus*
Indian Leaf   *Kallima inachus*
Lapland Fritillary   *Euphydryas iduna*
Lapland Ringlet   *Erebia embla*
Large Blue   *Maculinea arion*
Large Chequered Skipper
    Heteropterus morpheus
Large Copper   *Lycaena dispar*
Large Heath   *Coenonympha tullia*
Large Skipper   *Ochlodes venatus*
Large Tortoiseshell
    Nymphalis polychloros
Large Wall Brown   *Lasiommata maera*
Large White   *Pieris brassicae*
Lesser Purple Emperor   *Apatura ilia*
Little Blue   *Cupido minimus*
Long-tailed Blue   *Lampides boeticus*
Lulworth Skipper   *Thymelicus acteon*
Marbled White   *Melanargia galathea*
Marsh Fritillary   *Eurodryas aurinia*
    formerly *Euphydryas*
Meadow Brown   *Maniola jurtina*
Monarch   *Danaus plexippus*
Moorland Clouded Yellow
    Colias palaeno
Mountain Ringlet   *Erebia epiphron*
Nettle Tree Butterfly   *Libythea celtis*
Northern Brown Argus
    Aricia artaxerxes
Orange Tip   *Anthocharis cardamines*
Owl Butterfly   *Caligo idomeneus*
Painted Lady   *Cynthia cardui*
Peacock   *Inachis io*
Pearl-bordered Fritillary
    Boloria euphrosyne
Plain Tiger   *Danaus chrysippus*
Postman   *Heliconius melpomene*
Purple-edged Copper
    Lycaena hippothoe
Purple Emperor   *Apatura iris*
Purple Hairstreak   *Quercusia quercus*
Red Admiral   *Vanessa atalanta*
Ringlet   *Aphantopus hyperantus*

Rock Grayling *Hipparchia alcyone*
Scarce Swallowtail
           Iphiclides podalirius
Scotch Argus *Erebia aethiops*
Short-tailed Blue *Everes argiades*
Silver-spotted Skipper
           Hesperia comma
Silver-studded Blue *Plebejus argus*
Silver-washed Fritillary
           Argynnis paphia
Small Blue *Cupido minimus*
Small Copper *Lycaena phlaeas*
Small Heath *Coenonympha pamphilus*
Small Pearl-bordered Fritillary
           Boloria selene
Small Skipper *Thymelicus sylvestris*
Small Tortoiseshell *Aglais urticae*

Small White *Pieris rapae*
Sooty Satyr *Satyrus ferula*
Southern Swallowtail
           Papilio alexanor
Speckled Wood *Pararge aegeria*
Swallowtail *Papilio machaon*
Tree Grayling *Hipparchia statilinus*
Turquoise Blue *Plebicula dorylas*
Two-tailed Pasha *Charaxes jasius*
Wall or Wall Brown
           Lasiommata megera
White Admiral *Ladoga camilla*
White-letter Hairstreak
           Strymonidia w-album
Wood White *Leptidea sinapis*
Woodland Ringlet *Erebia medusa*

Appendix IV   Scientific names of plants mentioned in the text

Alder Buckthorn *Frangula alnus*
Apple *Malus* species
Bilberry *Vaccinium myrtillus*
Bird's Foot *Ornithopus perpusillus*
Bird's-foot Trefoil *Lotus corniculatus*
Birthwort *Aristolochia clematitis*
Black Medick *Medicago lupulina*
Blackthorn *Prunus spinosa*
Bog Whortleberry
           Vaccinium uliginosum
Bramble *Rubus fruticosus*
Broom *Sarothamnus scoparius*
Buckthorn *Rhamnus catharticus*
Cabbage *Brassica* species
Charlock *Sinapis arvensis*
Cherry *Prunus* species
Clover *Trifolium* species
Corydalis *Corydalis* species
Cotton Grass
           Eriophorum angustifolium
Cowslip *Primula veris*
Cow Wheat *Melampyrum pratense*
Cranberry *Vaccinium oxycoccos*
Cuckoo Flower *Cardamine pratensis*
Damson *Prunus* species
Devil's-bit Scabious *Succisa pratensis*
Dogwood *Cornus sanguinea*
Dyer's Greenweed *Genista tinctoria*
Elm *Ulmus procera*

Fennel *Foeniculum vulgare*
Garlic Mustard *Alliaria petiolata*
Gorse *Ulex europaeus*
Great Water Dock
           Rumex hydrolapathum
Hedge Mustard *Sisymbrium officinale*
Honeysuckle *Lonicera periclymenum*
Horseshoe Vetch *Hippocrepis comosa*
Kidney Vetch *Anthyllis vulneraria*
Knapweed *Centaurea* species
Lime *Tilia* species
Lucerne *Medicago sativa*
Mat Grass *Nardus stricta*
Milk Parsley *Peucedanum palustre*
Milkweed *Asclepias* species
Mountain Houseleek
           Sempervivum montanum
Mustard *Brassica* species
Nettle *Urtica dioica*
Nettle Tree *Celtis australis*
Oak *Quercus* species
Pear *Pyrus* species
Plantain *Plantago* species
Plum *Prunus* species
Primrose *Primula vulgaris*
Purple Moor Grass *Molinia caerulea*
Radish *Raphanus sativus*
Ragged Robin *Lychnis flos-cuculi*
Rock Rose *Helianthemum* species

Sainfoin *Onobrychis vicii folia*	Thyme *Thymus* species
Sallow *Salix* species	Tuberous Pea *Lathyrus tuberosus*
Saxifrage *Saxifraga* species	Violet *Viola* species
Scabious *Scabiosa* species	White Beaked Sedge
Silverweed *Potentilla anserina*	*Rhynchospora alba*
Sorrel *Rumex* species	Wild Carrot *Daucus carota*
Stonecrop *Sedum* species	Wild Strawberry *Fragaria vesca*
Storksbill *Erodium cicutarium*	Willow *Salix* species
Thistle *Cirsium* and *Carduus* species	Wych Elm *Ulmus glabra*

Appendix V   Useful addresses

Butterfly Monitoring Scheme Details from Institute of Terrestrial Ecology, Monks Wood Experimental Station, Abbots Ripton, Huntingdon, PE17 2LS
Lepidoptera Distribution Mapping Scheme Details from Biological Records Centre, Institute of Terrestrial Ecology (address above)
British Butterfly Conservation Society, Tudor House, Quorn, Nr Loughborough, Leics LE12 8AD
Royal Entomological Society of London, 41 Queen's Gate, South Kensington, London SW7
Amateur Entomologist's Society, 355 Hounslow Road, Hanworth, Middx
The British Entomological and Natural History Society, c/o The Alpine Club, 74 South Audley Street, London W1
S.E.L. Societas Europaea Lepidopterologica, c/o Landessammlungen für Naturkunde, Erbprinzenstrasse 13, D-7500 Karlsruhe 1, West Germany

Appendix VI   The nature photographers' code of practice

All photographers working in Britain should read a leaflet entitled: *The Nature Photographers' Code of Practice* produced by the Association of Natural History Photographic Societies. Copies can be obtained from the Royal Society for the Protection of Birds, The Lodge, Sandy, Bedfordshire SG19 2DL, by sending a stamped addressed envelope. The following section is relevant to butterfly photography:

'For cold-blooded animals and invertebrates, temporary removal from the wild to a studio or vivarium (or aquarium) for photography is a well-accepted practice, but subsequent release should be in the original habitat and as soon as practicable.

Chilling or light anaesthesia for quietening invertebrates is not recommended. If it is undertaken, subjects should only be released when the effects have completely worn off.

When microhabitats (e.g. tree-bark, beach rocks etc.) have been disturbed, they should be restored after the photography.

Insect photographers should be familiar with the Joint Committee for the Conservation of British Insects' *Code of Insect Collecting*. While this allows moderate rarities to be collected, photographers should take a restrictive view of what ought even to be put at risk by their activities.'

Further reading

Field guides for Europe

Higgins, L.G. and Riley, N.D. *A field guide to the Butterflies of Britain and Europe.* Collins, 1970. (paintings)

Hyde, G.E. *Spotter's Guide to Butterflies.* Usborne, 1978. (paintings)

Lyneborg, Leif. *Blandford Colour Series Butterflies.* Blandford, 1975. (paintings)

Whalley, Paul. *Hamlyn Nature Guide Butterflies.* Hamlyn, 1979. (photographs)

Field guides for Britain only

Carter, David J. *The Observer's Book of Caterpillars.* Warne, 1979. (paintings; includes advice on rearing)

Howarth, T.J. *South's British Butterflies.* Warne, 1973. (paintings; includes caterpillars)

Identification guides for plants

Clapham, A.R.; Tutin, T.G. and Warburg, E.F. *Flora of the British Isles.* Cambridge University Press, 1962. (keys, descriptions and some line drawings)

Fitter, R. and Blamey, M. *Wild Flowers of Britain and Northern Europe.* Collins, 1964. (paintings)

Hay, R. and Synge, P.M. *The Dictionary of Garden Plants in Colour.* Ebury Press and Michael Joseph, 1969. (photographs)

Martin, W. Keble. *The Concise British Flora.* Michael Joseph and Ebury Press, 1969. (paintings)

Mitchell, A. *A Field Guide to the Trees of Britain and Northern Europe.* Collins, 1974. (paintings)

Phillips, R. *Wild Flowers of Britain.* Ward Lock, 1977. (photographs)

General

Allen, David. *The Naturalist in Britain. A Social History.* Allen Lane, 1976; Penguin, 1978.

Dennis, R.L.H. *The British Butterflies, their origin and establishment.* E.W. Classey, 1977.

Dickson, Richard. *A Lepidopterist's Handbook.* Ed. P.W. Cribb. Amateur Entomologist's Society, 1976. (Mainly for collectors, but includes information on rearing Lepidoptera.)

Ford, E.B. *Butterflies.* New Naturalist Series. Collins, 1977.

Ford, R.L.E. *Practical Entomology.* Warne, 1963.

Goodden, Robert. *The Wonderful World of Butterflies.* Hamlyn, 1977.

Johnstone, R.F., Frank, P.W. and Michener, C.D. *Annual Review of Ecology and Systematics* Vol 6. Palo Alto Calif. 1975. See chapter *Butterfly Ecology* by Gilbert, L.E. and Singer, M.C.

Laithwaite, Eric; Watson, Alan and Whalley, Paul. *The Dictionary of Butterflies and Moths in Colour.* Michael Joseph, 1975.

Lees, J. Ferguson and Campbell, Bruce. *The Natural History of Britain and Northern Europe*. Hodder and Stoughton, 1978–1979. (Five volume guide to animals and plants arranged by habitat. Includes paintings of European butterflies.)

Matthews, Patrick. *The Pursuit of Butterflies and Moths: An anthology*. Chatto and Windus, 1957.

Measures, David. *Bright Wings of Summer*. Cassell, 1976.

Newman, L. Hugh. *Looking at Butterflies*. Collins, 1977.

Newman, L. Hugh. *Create a Butterfly Garden*. John Baker, 1967.

Sheail, J. *Nature in Trust, the History of Nature Conservation in Britain*. Blackie, 1976.

Smart, Paul. *The Illustrated Encyclopaedia of the Butterfly World*. Hamlyn, 1976.

Tinbergen, Niko. *Curious Naturalists*. Penguin Educational, revsd. edn. 1974.

Acknowledgements

Colour photographs

Aquila: M.A. Bushby 64, 100 top, E.A. Janes 63 top, 127 bottom; T. Leach 109 bottom, Duncan I. McEwan 61 bottom; Biofotos: Heather Angel 36 top, 73 bottom, 74 bottom, 91 top, 110 bottom, Jeremy Thomas 35; British Museum (Natural History) 17; Geoff du Feu 92, 109 top; Jill Fry 63 bottom, 73 top; John Mason 36 bottom, 74 top, 91 bottom; David Parker 127 top; Premaphotos Wildlife: R.A. Preston-Mafham 61 top; Bryan L. Sage 62; Paul Whalley 18.

Black-and-white photographs

Ardea: I.R. Beames 29 left, Su Gooders 70; Aquila: E.A. Janes 71, Richard T. Mills 31; Biofotos: Heather Angel 19, 20, 21, 22, 24, 29 right, 59, 68, 72, 76, 84, 85, 97, 98, 99, 100 bottom, 103, 123, 125, Jeremy Thomas 34; Cyril Clarke 13; Courtauld Institute of Art 10; Nigel Gardener 82; John Mason 30, 32, 75, 101; Natural History Photographic Agency: Stephen Dalton 77; Premaphotos Wildlife: K.G. Preston-Mafham 33, 100 top; F.A. Urquhart 87; Alyson Whalley 8, 86; Paul Whalley 93.

The photograph on page 8 is reproduced by courtesy of the Trustees of the British Museum.

The photograph on page 10 is reproduced by courtesy of the Courtauld Institute of Art.

The photograph on page 17 is reproduced by courtesy of the Trustees of the British Museum (Natural History).

The map on page 136 is reproduced by courtesy of the Biological Records Centre, Institute of Terrestrial Ecology, Monks Wood Experimental Station.

Index

Page references in italic refer to illustrations; page references in bold refer to individual life-histories in Appendix 1.